CHILDREN MAKING BOOKS

A range of cover patterns

Children Making Books

LESLIE BENNETT

JACK SIMMONS

A & C Black · London

First published 1978
A & C Black Ltd
35 Bedford Row, London WC1R 4JH
© 1978 Leslie Bennett and Jack Simmons
ISBN 0 7136 1893 0

Bennett, Leslie
   Children making books.
   1. Book design – Study and teaching
   2. Bookbinding – Study and teaching
   I. Title   II. Simmons, Jack
   372.5   Z116.A3
   ISBN 0-7136-1893-0

Filmset and printed in Great Britain by
BAS Printers Limited, Over Wallop, Hampshire

Contents

Photographs

Foreword

In Priscilla Johnston's biography of her father, Edward Johnston – the greatest of all English calligraphers – she tells how he suggested that she should write a book for her mother's birthday. 'I was five years old', she says, 'and saw no difficulty in such a project, so I readily agreed. The first essential was, of course, a book; clearly you cannot write a book until you have a book to write in. He got out a big sheet of what was probably hand-made paper and showed me how to fold it in folio, quarto, octavo, and how to cut the pages . . .'

That surely is the point. Following a graded course in bookcrafts and making books *in vacuo*, so to speak, is a sterile business without a positive purpose and therefore often devoid of joy and of that sense of celebration that is appropriate to the completion of a book made for some pressing reason. Equally dispiriting is the situation where a child needs a book in which to record his findings or for some other urgent purpose, but he does not know the simple traditional ways of making one. They should be part of every child's heritage, so that the construction of books is a normal, regular practice.

It is this attitude of mind to the craft of book production that is stressed in this manual; it is seen as an integral part of children's environment. There are no gimmicks: the time-honoured methods of the bookbinder are handed down with clarity and a sense of pleasure in their use. Children making books is as natural as children making pictures or children making music.

Robin Tanner
Old Chapel Field
February 1977

Acknowledgements

Our grateful thanks are due to the following people, who have helped us in various ways.

To Aileen Burton, Ian Bennett and Richard Howard, who read and commented upon the manuscript.

To Susan Curtis who typed the manuscript.

To Amy Simmons who typed the amendments for the final draft.

To John Simmons who took some of the photographs.

To the children of St. Christopher's C.E. School, Langford, Oxfordshire, who made most of the books and who appear in the photographs that illustrate these pages.

To the hundreds of teachers and primary school children who have shared with us the challenge and delight of making books, and who led us to the point of making this one.

Our special thanks are given to Robin Tanner, firstly for writing the foreword, and more especially for his constant encouragement, wise counsel and unfailing support to us and to countless numbers of teachers and children for so many happy years.

Leslie Bennett
Jack Simmons

Introduction

In many infants schools concern for writing begins, one
might say, with the making of books.

A Language for Life (HMSO 1975, para. 5.22)

Since man has inhabited the earth he has found ways of leaving
his mark. Using whatever materials were at hand he has
commented upon and recorded his way of life by painting the
walls of his cave, indenting the earth at his feet, knotting
coloured threads or notching sticks, incising stone or inscribing
the surfaces of clay or wax tablets.

As his purpose developed from the urge simply to record, to
the wish to communicate his thoughts to others, and to consider
theirs, the need to find ways to keep his graphic attempts in a
coherent manner led him to seek materials that could more
easily be stored and transported. Five thousand years ago the
Egyptians discovered that the reed papyrus could be persuaded
to yield thin sheets from which a flexible roll of any length
could be constructed. A stick or cane at each end of the length
enabled the reader to roll the papyrus from one to the other as
he read. Soon it became the practice to write in short lines and in
columns, instead of long lines from one end of the roll to the
other, so that the reader was not repeatedly rolling the entire
papyrus from one stick to the other. These rolls or 'volumen'
were often stored in cylindrical cases, and where several were
parts of a larger work they were kept together in a jar.

The development of parchment, attributed to Eumenes II of
Pergamus, two thousand years ago, resulted in a great advance
in book making. The skins of sheep and goats, cured and
skilfully scraped on both sides, provided a flexible and
sympathetic surface for the scribes. Calf-skin, treated in the
same way, became vellum. Rolled sheets, like the volumen,
proved awkward to handle and deteriorated rapidly in use, and
the folded book was devised. Each sheet was folded once, and
when several folded sheets were held together with stitching the
columns of writing on each leaf were accessible quickly and
easily. It was not long before several of these stitched sections of
a few sheets were put together and held in place by taking the

thread round a long strip of leather at the back. The same method of flexible sewing is still used today in hand-made bookbinding, and cannot be improved upon.

By the fifth century the binding had been adapted to produce the codex. Uniformly sized leaves of parchment or papyrus were secured by thread between wooden boards which in turn were covered, often with leather, and decorated. Basically the craft of book construction has changed little since then. The development of new materials, and particularly of paper, has led to a gradual refinement of techniques, but the traditional methods are still used to produce by hand, books that are highly valued as examples of fine craftsmanship.

Making books with children involves so much more than a mere exercise in handicraft. It demands a great deal of communication between children and teachers and between the children themselves. The necessity for a precise use of the vocabulary of book making is understood as they learn to distinguish between 'needles' and 'pins'; 'thread', 'cotton' and 'string'; 'paper' and 'cardboard'. They learn that every stage of the construction is important, and that the final product only really pleases when each step has been accomplished with care. They learn to be patient, for each stage has to be allowed its rightful share of time. They learn to choose and discriminate as they select materials, colours, and textures for the task they are beginning. The materials and tools themselves impose rules and disciplines upon the children, and demand the learning of many skills. Frequently a stage in the process will require two children to work in harmony together, and they learn to co-operate in the traditional context of the craftsman's workshop.

Through the use of eyes and hands, the most important tools of all, and through touching, holding and closely observing, the children learn to appreciate what is good, natural and sincere. Their involvement with the materials leads them to an understanding of the beauty of simplicity in form and colour. And when, finally, the book that they have made sits in their hands fresh from the press, there is a powerful incentive to fill it with good things. The book represents a confluence of many skills – the craftsman, the binder, the scribe, the artist, and the author – and they all reside in each child.

BOOKS WITH PAPER COVERS

CHAPTER I

A First Book

This very simple book involves only the skills of folding and sewing, using three holes and two stitches.

STEP 1: Take a piece of paper of such a size that, after three successive folds, the leaves will be a little larger than the required size of the finished book (e.g. a piece of paper of size A1 is reduced by folding to size A4).

Fold the paper once; fold the doubled sheet again. These four thicknesses must then be folded yet again. This forms the leaves. All folding must be as accurate as possible. This keeps the waste to a minimum, since less needs to be trimmed from the edges at the end of the work.

STEP 2: Take another piece of paper of a different colour, at least twice as big as the folded leaves, and fold it once. This piece, when placed around the outside of the folded leaves, forms the cover.

STEP 3: Open the book to the middle and mark three small dots on the centre crease – one in the middle and two more equidistant from the first, and not closer than 25 mm to the head and tail (see Figs. 1 and 2). Push a suitably sized needle through each dot (Fig. 2). These are 'holding' needles. Cut a piece of thread, the length of which is twice the distance between the two outside dots, plus 150 mm.

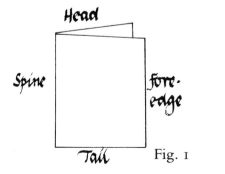

Fig. 1

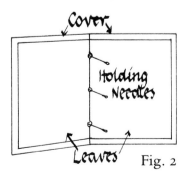

Fig. 2

Children working together: sewing

Normally, one would use bookbinder's needles and thread (size 16's medium) but for young and very inexperienced children it is better to use a needle with a big eye, and thick embroidery cotton.

With a partner to hold the book firmly, thread the middle needle and pull through until about 50 mm of thread is left inside the book.

Withdraw the holding needle at the head of the book, and pass the thread through in its place from the outside.

Remove the holding needle at the tail and pass the thread through to the outside.

Then pass the thread back through the middle hole to the inside, and take the needle off the thread. The book will now be sewn up as in Fig. 3.

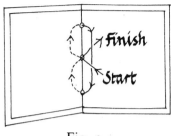

Fig. 3

STEP 4: Gently pull the two loose ends of thread to tighten the sewing. Pull up or down but not at right angles to the spine as this could lead to tearing. Having made sure that the two ends are one each side of the long centre stitch, tie a reef knot. Trim the ends of the thread to within 20 mm of the knot. The stitches should lie straight along the spine.

STEP 5: The book must now be trimmed so that the sides are parallel and all four corners square. If very thin, the book may be trimmed with a pair of large scissors or paper shears. Otherwise the card cutter may be used. Children will need to be quite confident and skilled before they can use the traditional tools for trimming – the knife and straight-edge.

CHAPTER 2

Towards Craftsmanship – 1

Folding

It will be noticed that after the first fold is made in the paper used for the leaves, subsequent folds become more and more difficult to carry out neatly as the thickness increases. Nevertheless, the temptation to slit the folds as the work proceeds must be avoided. Leaving the folds intact and using three separate holding needles to pierce the holes, helps to hold the whole book still and steady while the sewing proceeds, lessening the possibility of the threaded needle not going cleanly through the prepared holes, so forming a 'pepper-pot' appearance round each hole on the spine.

The present change from Imperial to Metric measures has carried away the historic names of paper sizes, and the traditional terms for the folded sizes of full sheets. When a full sheet was folded once, it was called FOLIO; folded twice it became QUARTO; and successive folds gave OCTAVO and SEXTODECIMO. These were written briefly as FOL., 4to, 8vo and 16mo. Thus the instructions in Step 1, Chapter 1, page 3, would have read: 'Fold a sheet of LARGE POST in quarto (4to), to give a finished book of 16 pages about $10\frac{1}{2}$" × $8\frac{1}{4}$" untrimmed.' (See Appendix D, page 114).

Trimming

The teacher can decide how far the making of a book shall be a precise mathematical exercise. To aid those children who have not yet mastered sufficient measuring skill, a cardboard template could be prepared, round which they could draw to mark the finished dimensions of their books. Trimming is then carried out along the pencil lines.

Testing

To test the quality of the completed work, hold up the book by the covers to the light. Little or no daylight should show

Fig. 4

between the cover and the leaves (Fig. 4). A space would mean that the sewing is loose, in which case, untie the knot, pull and tighten the stitches and re-tie the knot.

Anyone who can make a simple, single-section, three-hole sewn, flush-trimmed book, as described in detail above, has mastered the basic technique of book making. It is called 'single-section' because the whole book is made of a single sewn unit; 'three-hole' because it is sewn with two stitches through three holes; and 'flush-trimmed' because the covers and leaves are trimmed in one operation to the same size.

Look at a book from the reading corner, and you will find that in most cases it is multi-sectioned, and that the boards (i.e. the stiff back and front covers) project slightly beyond the leaves at the head, tail and fore-edge. The spine is protected by a strong binding of linen book-cloth, or in the case of older books, of leather. Paperbacks are as the name implies, and are usually flush-trimmed. One reason why they are cheap is the economy effected by the use of paper only, no expensive cardboard, linen or leather being used.

Making Paste

In order to progress beyond this basic book, it is necessary to become familiar with mixing and using cold-water paste, the most useful of all adhesives in making books. The preparation is very important. The paste powder must be stored in an airtight container, together with a dry spoon.

To make up the paste, half fill a clean container with cold water, adding the powder to it a teaspoonful at a time, and stirring continuously to avoid lumps forming. The finished paste for most jobs should be the consistency of thick cream which will just flow slowly from the tilted spoon. The spoon stored with the paste powder must always be kept quite dry, and not used to stir the paste. Paste is best left for 10–15 minutes after mixing, before it is used. Mixed paste does not keep well, so try always to mix just sufficient for immediate needs. A spot or two of antiseptic fluid will keep the mixed paste in good condition longer.

For thinner paste for such work as 'Paste Sandwiches', mix first as above and then add more water until the right consistency is reached. (See page 72).

CHAPTER 3

Developments of the Basic Book

A. SHAPED BOOKS

A variation in trimming the basic book can be carried out by trimming it to a pre-determined shape other than rectangular.

For example, a book about mathematical shapes could be trimmed to a hexagon; a book about food to the shape of an apple, orange or pear (Fig. 5).

Since trimming to this kind of shape must be done with scissors, it can be done only on a very thin book of a few leaves – perhaps just four and the cover. Furthermore, care must be taken not to cut the stitches when trimming.

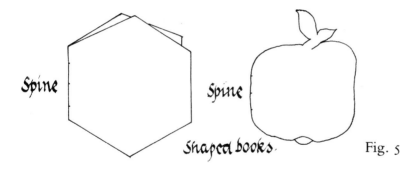

Shaped books.   Fig. 5

Thicker books could be made by folding each sheet separately and cutting it to shape. For accuracy, it is necessary to use a template, and to take care with the sewing which will be more difficult with separate loose leaves.

B. COVER PAPERS FOR SIMPLE BOOKS

A simple book can be made more interesting by decorating the cover paper before sewing it to the leaves (Step 2). Alternatively, a piece of patterned paper, 25 mm smaller all the way round than the cover, may be stuck on the front cover AFTER the book has been trimmed (see Fig. 6), and allowed to dry under pressure, as described on page 13, Step 6.

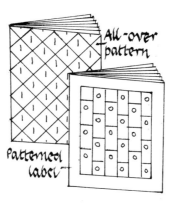

Fig. 6

Whenever a patterned cover paper is needed, it should be made as the first step, so that ink, paint or other wet media may be thoroughly dry before the cover paper is incorporated into the book. It is very frustrating to be making a book, and then be obliged to suspend the manufacture because the cover paper is not made, or is not ready to use. (For suggestions on making patterned cover papers, see Chapters 14 and 15.)

C. FLYLEAVES AND ENDPAPERS, COLOURED OR WHITE

The first and last leaves of a completed book should always be left blank as flyleaves. In order to leave sufficient pages as work pages, an extra sheet of paper (coloured or white) may be folded round the leaves before the cover is added. It is important that, if coloured paper is used, it should tone with the colour of the cover. The page next to the flyleaf will become the title page. (See Chapter 16 – Page Layout, Handwriting and Titles.)

The difficulty now arises that any additional leaves make the book thicker and therefore harder to pierce with the holding needles, prior to sewing. In this case a bookbinder's awl may be necessary to start the holes before inserting the holding needles. An awl is a sharp-pointed tapering spike, of round or square

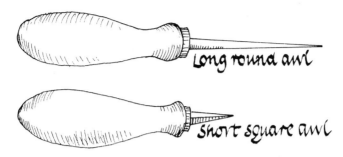

Long round awl

Short square awl

Fig. 7

section, fitted with a wooden handle (Fig. 7). Great care must be exercised in using this tool. It must be pressed and rotated very gently, so that there is no danger of a sudden piercing, which might stab an unwary hand. Only the extreme tip of the awl need pierce the book, keeping the hole small enough to grip the subsequent holding needle tightly.

When not in use the point of the awl should be protected with a large cork. Remember that Louis Braille was blinded by such an instrument. There are two ways by which a book may be safely pierced with an awl:

1   The book can be laid open and flat on a piece of waste wood or thick cardboard, and the awl pressed downwards into it.

2   When enough confidence and skill are acquired, the book may be held in one hand with the fingers well spread on each side of the spine outside, and the thumb inside, close to the mark where the hole will be made, while the other hand uses the awl from the inside of the book.

Bearing all this in mind, if coloured flyleaves are to be added to the book, the paper to be used will need to be twice the size of the cover, so that when it is folded and placed round the leaves,

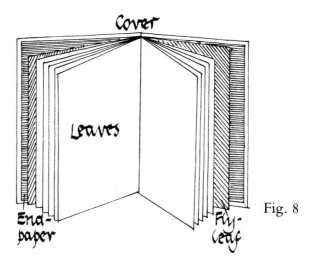

Fig. 8

it will give a flyleaf and endpaper at the beginning and end of the book (Fig. 8).

To make the cover strong, the cover paper may, after sewing, be pasted to the endpaper. When this has been done, the book must be allowed to dry thoroughly under light pressure before being trimmed. It will take at least forty-eight hours in a warm room; longer is better. Do not be impatient! The cover of a book trimmed while even slightly damp will subsequently curl and shrink, spoiling the whole job.

The correct technique for this piece of pasting is as follows:

1   Lay the book on a pile of single sheets of waste paper bigger than the book itself.
2   Place a sheet of waste paper between the flyleaf and the endpaper to be pasted, to act as a pasting guard protecting the rest of the book from stray paste.
3   Load a LARGE brush generously with paste and apply it to the endpaper brushing firmly and evenly in the direction of the arrows, i.e. outwards only (Fig. 9).
4   Lightly press the cover paper on to the now pasted endpaper. Remove the pasting guard and the top sheet of waste paper carefully, and finish smoothing down the cover.

Take the brush over the edges and on to the pasting guard.

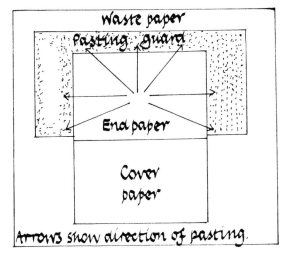

Fig. 9

5 Repeat the process for the other end of the book.
6 Allow the book to dry under light pressure. One or two large books are ideal as weights, or a board surmounted by one or two bricks. A manufactured standing press can be used, but it must not be screwed down too tightly.
7 Trim the book.
Before pressing, insert a 'pressing tin', a piece of waterproof paper or kitchen foil between the dry leaves and those just pasted. A piece of clean waste paper should be placed on each side of the waterproof paper, and another placed round the outside of the book (five pieces in all). These precautions will ensure that the dampness does not penetrate the dry parts, causing stretching and wrinkling.

If more than one book is to be pressed, it is necessary to stack the books very carefully and exactly on top of each other, since the edge of one book could make a dent in another, if carelessly stacked at different angles. If available, a pressing tin or piece of thick card between each book and the next will ensure even flat pressure. Books being pressed must always rest on a perfectly flat surface.

CHAPTER 4

More Simple Books – Unsewn

A. ZIG-ZAG OR CONCERTINA BOOKS

A zig-zag book is one made from a long strip of paper folded in zig-zag fashion. This is a book that requires no sewing, but the folding must be very carefully done, if a neat result is to be achieved.

The steps in making a zig-zag book are as follows:

STEP 1: Prepare the cover papers.

STEP 2: Take a sheet of A1 paper and fold it once lengthwise (Fig. 10). Cut into two pieces.

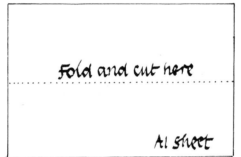

Fig. 10

STEP 3: Fold each piece in half, then fold each end back to the middle (Fig. 11).

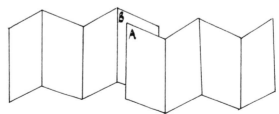

Fig. 11

STEP 4: Stick A to B, making a long zig-zag strip of seven leaves. Great care is necessary in sticking these pages, in order to keep the folds parallel. A may be pasted to B and

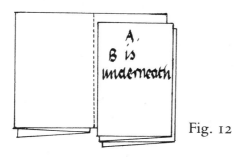

Fig. 12

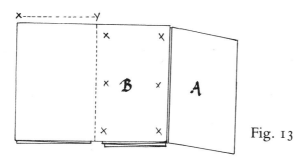

Fig. 13

dried under light pressure as previously described, or an alternative method may be used, which is helpful for younger or less skilful fingers.

Place the two folded pieces together as in Fig. 11. 'Knock up' the leaves straight and square, and lay them folded on the table. Without letting them slip or move, open to the joining pages (Fig. 12). Get a partner to hold side 1 quite still. Hold side 2 yourself. Lift leaf A and put a few spots of quick drying adhesive on B as shown by the crosses in Fig. 13.

Still keeping both parts steady, fold A back on to B and press down. It will stick almost immediately. The zig-zag of seven leaves, one of double thickness, is now complete.

STEP 5: Trim the two cover papers to the exact WIDTH of the folded leaves (x–y, Fig. 13). The covers should be a little longer than the leaves.

15

STEP 6: Paste and attach covers, and allow to dry under light pressure.

STEP 7: Trim the head and tail of the book. The sides cannot be trimmed, of course, because the folds occur here. This is why the folding must be as accurate as possible, and why the cover papers must be trimmed to width before attaching. One advantage of a zig-zag book is that it will stand on a table, showing the whole contents of each complete side.

Children like to make zig-zag books as a change from the sewn variety, and having once learnt the process, they need almost no help or supervision, apart from a reminder about accurate folding.

B. CONTINUOUS BOOKS

This is a variation of the zig-zag book, where the pages fold in the same direction instead of in alternate directions, and where the first and last pages join to make a continuous book that has no beginning and no end. It is a very suitable construction for books about those natural phenomena that follow a sequence of events in a cycle – the seasons, the life of animals or plants, etc. In making such a book children are helped to understand fundamental ideas about the world, and to acquire concepts of time and change within the rhythmic pattern of events.

The number of pages in such a book depends upon the number of stages in the cycle, for each page will represent one stage. For example, a book about the seasons would need four pages, one each for Winter, Spring, Summer and Autumn (Fig. 14). A book about a bird observed in the school grounds might need six pages, to represent the stages of nest building, laying eggs, hatching the eggs, feeding the young, flying from the nest and mating.

Since the book is free-standing and will be handled a lot it is best constructed in thin card, though good-quality cartridge paper can also be used. Having decided upon the number of pages, their dimensions and the most suitable material, proceed with the construction as follows.

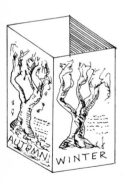

Fig. 14

16

Fig. 15

Take a piece of card or paper long enough for the number of pages required plus one. For some books it will be necessary to join two pieces of card end to end by the overlapping of two pages as described in Fig. 12. Measure accurately and, using a straight-edge and a bone folder, score the card as shown in Fig. 15. (See also the photographs on page 24.) A straight-edge is a heavy ungraduated metal ruler. Fold along the score lines (Fig. 16) and using quick-drying adhesive, stick the back of page A to page B.

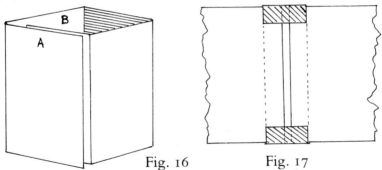

Fig. 16   Fig. 17

A variation in construction, which calls for greater skill and will appeal to many competent young bookbinders, is to cut each page separately and join the pages together with book-linen hinges (Fig. 17). The inside of each hinge is covered with a strip of linen, and the bone folder used to press it against the edges of the card. Making the last join, to complete the continuous book, is a test of the bookbinder's skill in mastering his materials and tools.

17

C. A SIMPLE LOOSE-LEAF FOLDER

Some separate leaves placed inside a folded cover paper and laced in place, is the basic idea of all loose-leaf folders. There are no great difficulties to be faced in making such a folder.

STEP 1: Prepare cover papers if desired.

STEP 2: Decide the size and number of leaves required, and prepare same.

STEP 3: Choose a piece of stout paper or thin card (manilla is by far the best, as it folds sharply without fraying or spoiling) which when folded will be 10 mm wider and longer than the leaves (e.g. leaf size 200 × 150 mm, cover size 210 × 320 mm). The cover will have a margin of 5 mm all round the leaves. The leaves and cover could be cut exactly the same size, but if the leaves were not quite aligned, they would show outside the cover and give an untidy appearance.

STEP 4: Attach cover papers (if made).

STEP 5: Choose a piece of paper for a flyleaf, cut to the same size as the leaves. At 15 mm from the left-hand side, mark and pierce two or three holes according to the size of the book, for lacing in the finished leaves. In the case of just a few leaves, these may be pierced in one operation together with the flyleaf, but if the number of leaves is such that they must be pierced in two or more lots, or if it is desired to add more leaves at a later date, then the flyleaf may be used as a template, achieving correct alignment for all the contents. The flyleaf is also used to mark the correct position of the holes in the back cover (Fig. 18). Punch-pliers are useful for making clean holes.

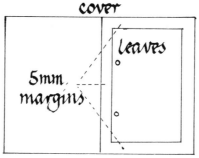

Fig. 18

Lacing

If two holes are used, the ends of a piece of cord are threaded through the back cover from the outside, passed through the leaves and flyleaf, and tied on top of the flyleaf. If the pages are all complete, the cord should be tied in a reef knot and then again in a bow. If the cord tends to fray, knot the ends, or dip the tips in glue. In the case of three holes, thread a large rugmaking needle with the cord, and follow the pattern of three-hole sewing. For a temporary lacing, any piece of soft string will do, tied through the top and bottom holes in a bow.

To make a stronger flyleaf, glue a strip of manilla to the left-hand edge. Gummed linen washers are available for reinforcing the holes in the leaves.

When making pages for a loose-leaf folder, it must be remembered that about 20 mm of the left-hand side of every leaf will be hidden under the lacing, and therefore this amount must be added to the margin on that side when the page is set out (Fig. 19). If using both pages of the leaf, the extra margin will occur on the right-hand side of the back of the leaf.

Fig. 19

Similarly, if it is decided to bind some existing pages into a loose-leaf folder, the results will not be very satisfactory if there is not the usual margin plus 20 mm on the left-hand side of every leaf. If not, the only remedy is to paste an extra strip, 20 mm wide, to each leaf separately, overlapping by 5 mm.

This may be an exacting task, but paste is the bookbinder's most useful material. Self-adhesive transparent tape may appear to offer a quicker and easier method, but it is not a satisfactory medium. Apart from the fact that children are inclined to get it in a tangle, the edges of Sellotape eventually show as a dirty line, or else adhere to the next page.

A second method of making a simple loose-leaf folder is to use two separate covers, in which case holes must be punched through both, and the lacing taken through the front cover where it will show. The colour of the cord must agree well with the colour of the folder, of course.

Then, in order that the front cover may fold back easily to reveal the contents, it will be necessary to put a fairly sharp crease in it. This is done by placing a straight-edge on the cover about 20 mm from the left-hand edge and running a bone folder or some similar blunt and smooth instrument down it to make an indentation or score-mark. Keeping the ruler in place and using the bone folder, press the cover back against it. It will fold easily on the score-mark, and the fold may be completed with the flat of the bone folder (see photograph, page 24). Smooth the cover flat again, and thereafter it will fold back easily on the mark.

CHAPTER 5

Towards Craftsmanship – 2

Sewn Book or Loose-Leaf?
Which is better? Each has its own advantages, and meets different needs.

Many children prefer a sewn book, because it seems to them a 'real' book, but an accident with a bottle of ink or a jar of dirty painting water could ruin a whole book by spoiling just one page. A leaf taken out can never be disguised, and even if the opposite leaf in the section is removed to match, this loosens the sewing sufficiently to rob the book of its taut neatness.

This problem of spoilt pages can be overcome by making the leaves of the same coloured paper as the flyleaves and endpapers. The written work is then done on writing paper, and when the finished page is considered satisfactory, it can be attached to the coloured page with five MINUTE blobs of quick-drying adhesive (like Copydex). It is sufficient to put a blob 20 mm away from each corner and one in the middle. Paste must NOT be used in this case, since it will soak into the coloured paper and make wrinkles, and will also soak, discolour and blotch any ink writing. A small dab of stiff mountant paste is satisfactory, however.

Choosing a Colour
The custom of making the leaves of a book from coloured paper, and attaching the work pages to them, is very popular with children. Great care is needed in the choice of colours offered to the children. Black, grey, fawn, any neutral or dull colour, give the most satisfactory results, because they form a suitable background to the children's work pages. Garish colours can be overpowering. In fact, colour should be the first thing discussed by the teacher and children when starting to make a book. 'What colour', asks the teacher, 'would you like to make your book?' (Note the SINGULAR.) Then, through

discussion, steps should be taken to ensure that the book covers, endpapers, book-cloth, etc. are all made in harmonious colours which complement the original choice. Many well-made books have not been attractive or successful, because different parts have been made from discordant colours. Would anyone want to buy a photograph album with fluorescent lime-green leaves? How would coloured photographs look, mounted on this? The use of colour is so often neglected in children's education. It is said that children like bright colours, and should therefore be allowed to use them. Yes, but not indiscriminately. Supposing a child has chosen yellow as the main colour for his book. From that point he will probably need help in keeping his choice in mind as he selects colours for his book-cloth or endpapers, or covers. It will help him if he is asked to list all the colours he knows that have yellow in them – greens, oranges, buffs, browns – and then to experiment with different combinations from that list until he is pleased with his final choice. This process of selection can often become a subject for discussion and the sharing of views between a group of children.

Careful thought and careful choice are two most important elements of the children's work. The subtleties and interest of natural colours should never be overlooked. Let us always study intently the colours of nature. Is a stone always a dull lifeless grey or brown? How many individually different pebbles make up the general colour of the beach? How many colours are there on the bark of a silver birch? Let us look twice at 'mud' colours. And let us see how many myriad shades and tints can be obtained from one primary colour.

Powder paint, straight from the tin, is raw and crude. The addition of a little white or black, or both, can give a much more interesting effect. With small children there is a strong case for using primary colours as they are, but usually because the children are still, perhaps, learning to name the colours, or to find out what results from mixing them. Even so, when making our first books, we can make sure the book itself is neutral in colour, so that a cover paper in, say, red, blue and purple looks well on it.

CHAPTER 6

Work Envelopes

Before going on to more advanced types of books, there are advantages in making a large envelope or work-holder. A large, strong envelope is most useful for safely holding all the parts of an unfinished book. It is very frustrating to be making a book only to find that a carefully prepared cover paper is missing, perhaps accidentally gathered up with the waste, or stepped on and spoilt!

Furthermore, when a book is finished, the envelope will make a good protective cover while the book is not in use.

An envelope may be made with no knowledge of measuring, but involving just the skills of cutting, folding and sticking. On the other hand, it may be made a mathematical exercise, if the teacher wishes it. The instructions that follow assume no measuring skill whatever, but do assume that the children are able to hold a ruler still while a pencil line is drawn along its edge.

STEP 1: Take half a sheet of manilla paper, approximately 380 mm × 520 mm. Place it on the table with the machine-cut edges on the left (Fig. 20). This size takes quite a lot of room, and most school tables and desks are not very big. A cover to place over two adjacent desk tops can be very simply made from hardboard (Chapter 18).

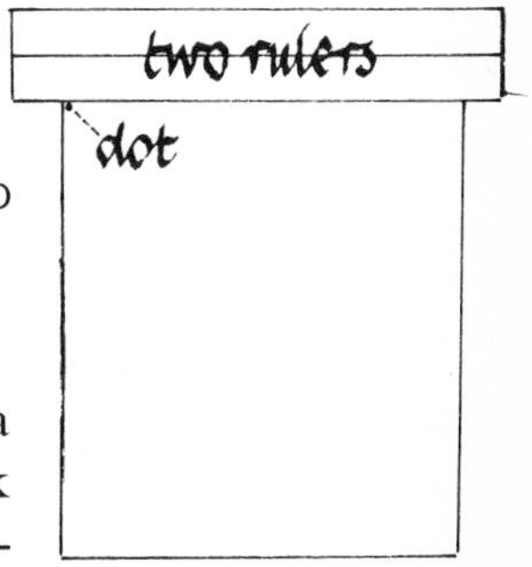

Fig. 20

two rulers

dot

Let the children work in pairs, making one envelope at a time, changing roles as craftsman and assistant when work is finished on the first envelope. Make a dot on the left-hand edge, two rulers' width from the top (Fig. 20).

Scoring

Folding up

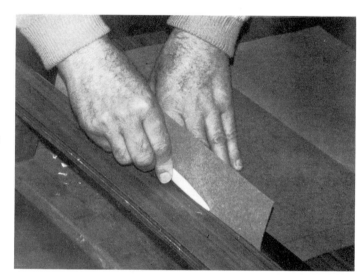

Finishing the fold

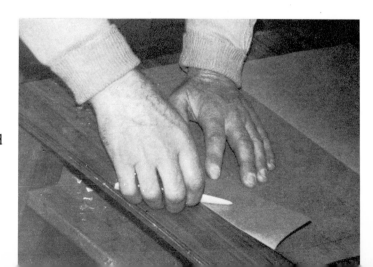

STEP 2: Fold the bottom edge up to the dot, ensuring that the left-hand edge is straight and accurate (Fig. 21). Crease the fold sharply with the flat of a bone folder, after starting the crease with a CLEAN finger.

Draw a line along the edge marked xy (Fig. 21).

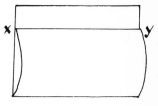

Fig. 21

STEP 3: The right-hand edge may now be trimmed (while folded) on the card cutter, with the creased edge at the top.

STEP 4: Open the work flat. Use the width of one ruler to draw the lines AB and CD (Fig. 22).

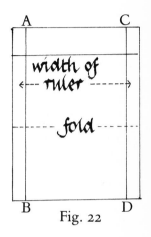

Fig. 22

STEP 5: Shade in the portions indicated in Fig. 23.

STEP 6: Cut away the shaded portions, keeping just inside lines EF and GH (as indicated by dots).

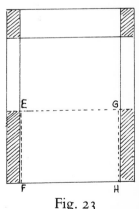

Fig. 23

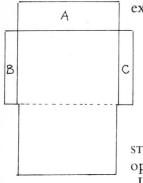

Fig. 24

STEP 7: The work will now look like Fig. 24. Fold sharply flaps A, B and C, using a ruler and bone folder, as explained on page 17.

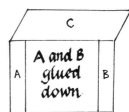

Fig. 25

STEP 8: Fold bottom part up into place. Leave A, B and C open.

Lightly glue A and B ONLY with quick-drying adhesive, and press into place. The envelope is completed (Fig. 25). Name, decoration or patterned label may be added as desired. If the cutting has been accurate, the envelope will lie quite flat without bulging when empty.

If the envelope is going to demand measuring skills from the children, then the following refinements, using a 30/60 degree set square, will add a more professional appearance to the finished article. Taper the parts shaded in Fig. 26. Cut away the shaded parts before gluing up. The cut-away portion on the lower edge of the diagram could be marked out by folding it into position and marking round the tops of flaps A and B. This cut-away makes easier the insertion and withdrawal of the contents of the envelope.

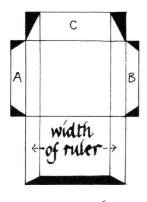

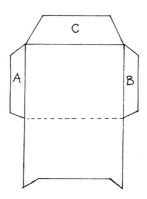

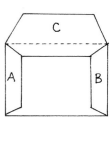

Fig. 26

BOOKS WITH CARDBOARD COVERS

Worktop prepared for pasting

CHAPTER 7

Zig-zag Book with Board Covers

When the covers of a book are cut from cardboard or strawboard, they are always referred to as 'the boards'. Boards make a book stronger and more durable; and by projecting 2 or 3 mm beyond the leaves greater protection is given to the contents.

Making a book with board covers demands some skill in measuring; it demands attention to detail and patience; it demands speedy work without haste, which calls for concentration and efficiency; and it demands an eagerness for fine craftsmanship. It is therefore an advantage if the children have already made the simpler books, and if younger, less experienced children have been watching and helping older, more experienced children making more advanced books. Such an apprenticeship is of great benefit when the older children give place to the younger. Older children pass on their knowledge with great pride and are very strict about following the rules. The younger children acquire knowledge very quickly in this way, and always appear to accept, without question, the necessary disciplines.

The zig-zag book with board covers is made as follows:

STEP 1: Prepare cover papers.

STEP 2: Prepare and trim the zig-zag leaves as described on pages 14 and 15.

STEP 3: Cut the boards to such a size that they are bigger by 5 mm than the prepared leaves, i.e. size of folded leaves 250 mm × 210 mm, then size of boards must be 255 mm × 215 mm.

STEP 4: Trim the cover papers so that they are 20 mm bigger all the way round than the boards. Attach the covers to the boards by the following method:

Children working together: pasting

a Lay one cover paper, face downward, on a pile of single sheets of clean waste paper. Paste generously and evenly all over, starting from the middle and brushing outward only, taking the brush over the edges and on to the waste paper. Avoid letting the cover paper move or paste will be transferred to the patterned side (see Fig. 27).

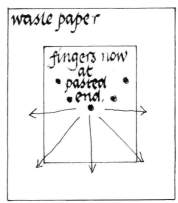

Fig. 27

The diagrams show that it is necessary to transfer the fingers of the free hand to the pasted portion, in order to paste the lower half of the cover paper.

b The pasting finished, lift up the pasted cover and with a partner's help, remove the top soiled sheet of waste, discard it at once, and place the cover paper back on the clean pile of waste. Wipe the fingers.

Work is bound to be spoiled if sticky sheets of waste paper remain on the work table for one second longer than is absolutely necessary. No paste should find its way to desks, tables, floor, clothes, faces, or up the brush handle. The sooner that the correct pasting technique is a habit, the better for everyone concerned. It is impossible to over-emphasise this point.

c Position the board on the cover paper with a 20 mm margin all round. Press the board firmly all over.

d Taking each corner in turn, fold the cover paper on to the board making a neat 45° angle and press down. Using the bone folder or a clean thumb nail (not too sharp) gently press the cover paper against the two edges of the corner of the board, where the dotted line is shown in Fig. 28. Apply a small dab of paste at x.

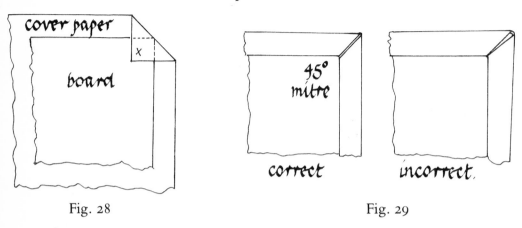

Fig. 28   Fig. 29

e Tightly fold the side flaps over, leaving no space whatever between paper and board (Fig. 29). Some children use their fingers to set the flaps over. Others use the top two or three sheets of the waste paper pile to pull the flaps over tightly. This latter method precludes any accidental tearing of the wet, pasted flaps. Rub the flaps down well.

STEP 5: Using pasting guards (see Fig. 30) paste the outside of the last zig-zag leaf. After discarding all sticky waste and wiping the fingers, lay the pasted leaf on the uncovered side of the board, leaving equal 2·5 mm margins on the three visible sides (Fig. 31). Rub down well.

STEP 6: To attach second board, paste the last leaf as before, fold the leaves to the closed position and place the board on the pasted leaf, aligning it exactly with the first board. It will be necessary to get right over the work to do this accurately.

Open the book and rub down well.

STEP 7: Dry under light pressure as previously described.

32

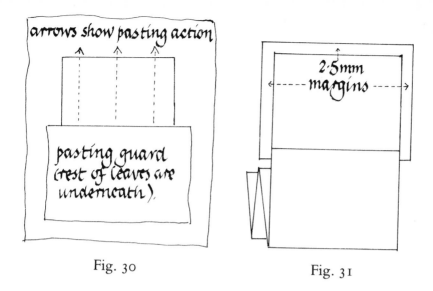

Fig. 30

Fig. 31

Once the cover papers are prepared, an experienced child, helped by a partner, can make a book like this in less than an hour. If, however, it is necessary to leave the work unfinished at any stage, then any parts which have been pasted must be kept under light pressure until required again. A board covered on one side only will warp and twist if left unpressed because of the expansion and contraction of the pasted paper.

It is, in fact, a sensible precaution to keep any newly-made book under a light weight on a flat surface for a week or more even when dry, all the time that it is not actually in use. Hot classrooms tend to warp new books, even when they seem to have dried satisfactorily. For the same reason, avoid putting books on window sills, or anywhere the sun may reach.

CHAPTER 8

Loose-leaf Folders with Board Covers

These may be of three types:

       I   Flexible Back
      II   Hard Back
     III   Open Back

I. Flexible Back

The steps in construction are:

STEP 1: Prepare cover papers.

STEP 2: Cut boards to such a size as to allow a margin of 2·5 mm all round over the size of the leaves. For example: leaf 250 × 200 mm, boards 255 × 205 mm.

STEP 3: Prepare three 'board linings', the same size as the leaves will be. Two of these will line the inside of the boards, as a kind of endpaper, while the third will be the flyleaf.

STEP 4: Cut two strips of book-cloth. The first piece should be the same length as the leaves, and about 80 mm wide. The second piece must be the length of the board plus 40 mm, by half the width of the board plus 20 mm. Fig. 32 shows sample measurements.

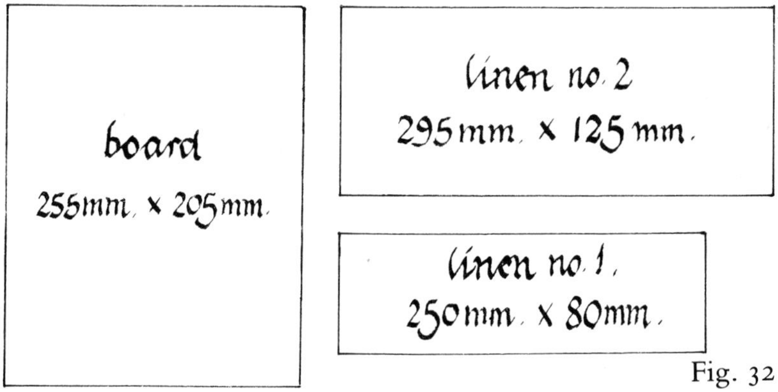

board

255mm × 205mm

linen no. 2

295mm × 125mm.

linen no. 1.

250mm × 80mm.

Fig. 32

Linen No. 2 makes the hinge of the folder. Linen No. 1 is the hinge lining.

STEP 5: Fold linen No. 2 in half lengthways to make a crease down the middle and then mark 5 mm each side of this middle crease, at the top and the bottom. Draw pencil lines through the marks. Draw another line 20 mm from the top. Work on the 'wrong' side of the linen, of course. See Fig. 33.

STEP 6: Paste the linen in the manner previously described, and place the boards in position as shown in Fig. 34.

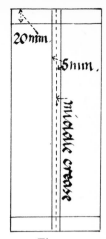

Fig. 33

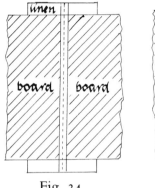

Fig. 34

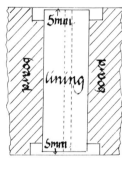

Fig. 35

STEP 7: Press the boards down well on to the linen. Wrap the 20 mm flaps tightly over the boards at the head and tail and rub down well. There will be a 10 mm space between the boards.

STEP 8: Paste the hinge lining and place it centrally over the space between the boards, thus lining the hinge (Fig. 35). Rub down well. Gently press the lining against the edge of the boards (dotted lines in Fig. 35). Turn the folder over and gently press the hinge itself against the edge of the boards. Use a bone folder or the rounded edge of a pair of scissors, but do it gently or the wet linen may be scored or torn. Rub the finger down the space between the boards to make the hinge and the lining adhere to each other.

At this stage, it is best to lay the folder aside under light pressure for 45–60 minutes, but work may proceed

35

immediately provided that care is taken not to disturb the edges of the still damp linen.

STEP 9: Measuring from the uncovered corners of the boards, make pencil marks that just overlap the edge of the linen hinge. All four measurements must be the same. If the hinge is not quite parallel with the fore-edge of the board, use the longest distance for all four marks, as shown in the exaggerated diagram of Fig. 36.

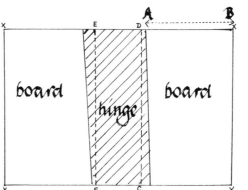

Fig. 36

If A to B is 168 mm make marks at C, D, E and F 170 mm from each corner (X). These marks are to ensure accurate alignment of the cover papers in the next step, so that the edge of the cover papers is parallel to the back of the folder, and is the same on both sides.

STEP 10: Trim the cover papers to this size:
LENGTH – length of board + 40 mm (the same length as linen No. 2).
WIDTH – X to C plus 20 mm.
Paste and attach cover papers placing the edge on marks C and D for side 1, and leaving a 20 mm margin or flap at the fore-edge, head and tail. Turn the folder over, rub down well and fold over the two corners and three flaps as described previously (pages 31–2, steps d and e). The second cover paper is similarly attached to side 2 using marks E and F.

36

STEP 11: Paste and attach board linings leaving a margin of 2·5 mm all round.

STEP 12: Open FLAT and allow to dry under light pressure. (N.B. Margins of 2·5 mm may be increased up to 5 mm but the bigger the margin, the less neat the finished result.)

STEP 13: Glue a 20 mm strip of card (manilla) to the left-hand edge of the flyleaf. Mark holes for lacing, and punch as described on page 18. Use the flyleaf as a template to mark the position of the holes on the back cover. Punch these holes with a 3 mm single-hole punch and fix eyelets with a hammer and eyelet tool, working on a piece of scrap wood or hardboard. Use the hammer only on a sturdy surface (see Fig. 37).

This completes the Flexible Back Folder. It is 'flexible' because the back is made of book-cloth.

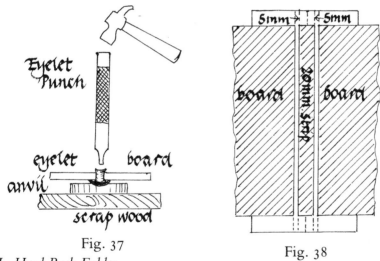

Fig. 37

Fig. 38

II. *Hard Back Folder*

This is made basically in the same way as the flexible back version, but the linen hinge and lining must be cut 20 mm wider, to accommodate a strip of board 20 mm wide and the same length as the board, and cut from the same material.

The hinge is marked out, and the three pieces of board attached, as shown in Fig. 38.

37

A partner's helping hand is most useful here, to hold steady the two boards and stiff back strip, while the hinge flaps at the head and tail are folded over.

When the hinge lining is put into place, it should be well rubbed down on the middle strip, then pressed against its edges with a bone folder. It must next be pressed against the edges of the cover boards, before the outer edges of the lining are finally rubbed down. Following this, the book must be turned over and the bone folder again applied to the 5 mm spaces from the back. This is to make the hinge and lining adhere to each other.

The cover papers and board linings, etc. are forwarded (attached and completed) as described for the flexible back.

III. Open Back Folder

To make an open back folder, each board must be bound separately with linen, a cover paper and a board lining in the proportions shown below in Fig. 39.

Eyeletted holes must be made in both boards, the lacing being taken right through and tied on the front board.

In order that the front cover board may open easily when the folder is laced up, a hinge must be made in it, while the back board remains in one piece (Fig. 40).

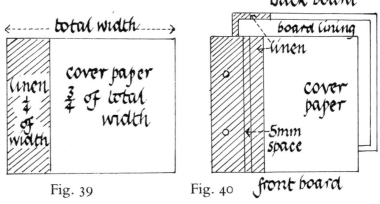

Fig. 39   Fig. 40

Previous experience should at this stage enable one to complete an open back folder without any further instruction. The marking out of the linen for the front cover board is shown in Fig. 41.

38

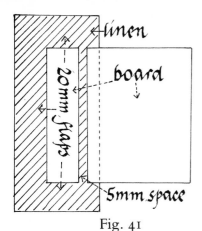

Fig. 41

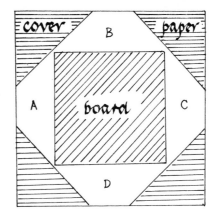

Fig. 42

As a matter of interest, the traditional method of covering the corners of a board with a cover paper is by mitring (see Fig. 42). The corners are marked with a 45° set square and cut off. The space between the corner of the cover board and the 45° line is equal to the thickness of the board. Flaps C and A are first turned over and rubbed down (Fig. 43). This gives a professional finish to the corner, but unless done perfectly, the corner of the board may show through a gap in the cover paper.

The method described previously on page 32, where the corners are left uncut and folded in first, is the method that children find best. It is, in fact, a method devised by some Oxfordshire teachers some years ago, and was arrived at through the experience of making books with children. It has proved almost foolproof, and is therefore strongly recommended.

Fig. 43a

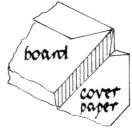

Fig. 43b

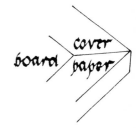

Fig. 43c

CHAPTER 9

Towards Craftsmanship – 3

The marking of the cover boards to ascertain the correct position for the placing of the cover papers (described in Fig. 36 as points C, D E and F) should be done on the extreme edge of the linen-covered boards, so that the pencil marks are unnoticeable on the finished article. Some children prefer to make these marks on the inside of the boards, and so the procedure for attaching the cover papers will be modified as follows. Instead of holding the pasted paper and lowering it into position on the board, the paper is left flat on the clean waste paper and the board is lowered on to it. This means that there is less handling of the pasted paper.

The best work is always done by the children who work in pairs, have their sleeves rolled up, and wear an apron with a large pocket. A piece of rag in the pocket is indispensable for keeping the fingers clean.

The importance of working with a partner has been mentioned several times. Children's readiness to co-operate with each other is precious. In a class of mixed ability and age, this co-operation is a great help to the teacher. More important, it helps the children to develop a sense of responsibility towards each other. The teacher may find, over a period, that a fine kind of apprenticeship is being built up, where the older or more skilful children are passing on their experience and skill to the younger, less skilful, less experienced children. They learn attitudes to work and to each other which benefit the atmosphere of the whole school.

Workmanlike appearance and attitudes, proper regard for tools and materials and the disciplines they impose, these are some of the valuable by-products of making books. Training the children to replace tools, clean and dry, in their proper place, so that they are always easy to find, maintains ship-shape and stable surroundings in which enthusiastic and thoughtful work can take place. The children must make it a habit to throw away useless waste, but to collect and store off-cuts and remainders of materials. Newspapers are available in almost limitless quantities, but strawboard, paper and linen are expensive and in short supply worldwide, so even small pieces are worth preserving. A piece of strawboard trimmed from a cover board may measure only 100 × 5 mm but it makes an excellent glue-spreader (see page 47). Spare pieces of coloured cover paper make excellent backgrounds for drawings in wax crayon. (Even the paste-covered newspaper will make papier-mâché if it is dropped into a little water in a bucket and allowed to soak.)

What a difference it makes to teachers if their children are thrifty, self-reliant and sensibly tidy both during their work and after it! Their effort and attention will then be given totally to the work in hand, and this is so much more important than mere cleverness. The amount of money that has to be spent on equipment will be much smaller as well-tended tools will last for years.

The effect of careful training on the attitudes of the children is as important as the actual work produced. Severe disciplinary trouble is unlikely to arise from children who can work confidently in an orderly atmosphere, and who have chosen and discussed their purposes.

Co-operation can accomplish much which competition cannot. Self-discipline means enjoyment, satisfaction and self-realisation. The children must know that their teacher is keenly interested in all that they are doing, and will not accept anything but their very best effort; yet constructive criticism and encouragement must dominate our approach to the children's work.

One of the teacher's dilemmas is to decide how much teaching to do, and when to leave the children alone to exercise their growing skills on self-directed tasks. There is no doubt that the techniques of using sharp tools – and they must be sharp, for blunt tools slip and are dangerous – must be carefully taught by demonstration and explanation. The children's practice with tools must be strictly supervised. Even when the children are proficient, frequent reminders may be necessary. It is when the techniques are familiar and being used by the children to express their own purposes, that the teacher must learn not to interfere, and run the risk of spoiling the spontaneity and essential child-like quality of the work. As an example, think of a child printing a cover paper with a lino-block. Teach him how to hold and use a lino tool; teach him the technique of printing; but having discussed the project with him, including the motif he has in mind, do not try to 'correct' his drawing, or make it look more as you have visualised it.

CHAPTER 10

Single-section Book with Board Covers, Quarter Bound

All books which are designated 'Quarter Bound' are so called because the back of the book, the spine, is covered with book-cloth, or bookbinder's linen which covers one quarter of the width of the book, the remaining three quarters being covered with a paper cover (see Fig. 39).

The construction is as follows:

STEP 1: Prepare cover papers.

STEP 2: Prepare leaves, flyleaves and endpapers.

STEP 3: Prepare a piece of MULL. This consists of a piece of bookbinder's muslin stuck to a piece of writing paper or cartridge paper with a flexible rubber glue, such as Copydex, or Bateman's. The finished size of this mull should be 50 mm wide by the length of the book minus 40 mm. It should be trimmed to size when thoroughly dry. A satisfactory substitute for the mull would be an odd piece of book-cloth or linen, the colour of which is immaterial since it will not show in the finished article. This is a good way to use up offcuts of book-cloth which are too small for other binding purposes.

STEP 4: Fold the mull in half lengthways and place it round the outside of the endpapers. Position it centrally on the spine so that the leaves are 20 mm longer at the head and tail (Fig. 44).

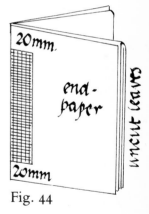

Fig. 44

STEP 5: If the leaves, etc. are left unslit as previously recommended, and the mull is attached at its extreme corners with the merest, minutest spot of rubber paste, the book will not slip or slide while it is sewn up. The sewing may be of the three-hole variety, but if the book is bigger than an exercise book, approximately 210 mm × 150 mm, five-hole sewing would be stronger (Fig. 45). In

Trimming, using the trimming press (see also page 104)

any case, the top and bottom holes should be not less than 25 mm from head and tail.

Providing that an odd number of holes is used, the method remains the same – start on the inside with the middle hole; proceed in and out to the top; then to the bottom, missing the middle hole on the way down; back to the middle where the sewing started; pulling tight and tying a reef knot over the long middle stitch. This prevents the knot from slipping back through the middle hole. Fig. 46 shows eleven-hole sewing as an example.

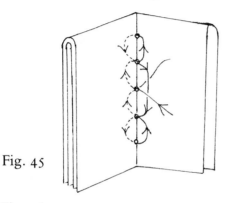

Fig. 45

Fig. 46

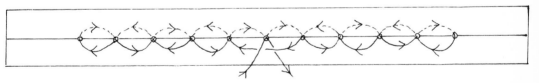

STEP 6: The book must now be trimmed, after marking the dimensions. Mark out the desired width first by measuring from the spine to the fore-edge. Then use a set-square on the fore-edge to mark the head and tail (Fig. 47).

STEP 7: If the book is very thin, it may be trimmed on the card cutter, but rarely does a card cutter give a completely clean edge. The most satisfactory tools for this task are a knife and straight-edge. Strong and steady pressure must be exerted on the straight-edge to keep it quite still, while the knife (very sharp) must be used with light, steady

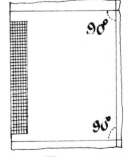

Fig. 47

45

Fig. 48

strokes, cutting through one leaf at a time. A 'trimming-press' is an excellent piece of apparatus to hold the book for trimming, and a home-made one is described in Chapter 18. Its advantage over a bought trimming press, apart from the saving in money, is that it will hold a much bigger book. All trimming must be done on a sheet of thick strawboard to protect the working surface.

STEP 8: Mark a line down the book, 5 mm from the spine (Fig. 48).

STEP 9: Cut the boards to such a size that, when placed on the line just drawn there is an overlap at the fore-edge, head and tail of 2·5 mm. If this measurement is too precise it may be adjusted to 3, 4 or 5 mm (maximum). Taking, as an example, a trimmed book size 210 × 150 mm, and using 2·5 mm as the margin of overlap, then the boards must be cut to 215 × 147·5 mm, but 0·5 mm is an extremely difficult measurement.

STEP 10: Release the corners of the mull, glued down in Step 5.

STEP 11: Attach the boards to the mull by one of these two methods:

a Traditional Method
Use pasting guards and paste (Fig. 49). Having pasted the mull, remove the pasting guard. Place the board on the

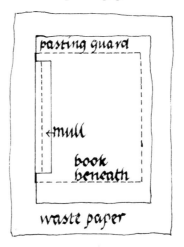

Fig. 49

line drawn on the mull, with equal margins at the head and tail. (The fore-edge margin will automatically come in the right position, of course.) Rub down well from the inside, supporting the open board on a book of similar thickness. When attaching the second board, lean right over the work so that it is possible to see clearly to align its corners with the corners of the first board. No line or measurements are therefore necessary on the second side of the book.

Allow to dry under pressure (remembering the waterproof and clean waste paper).

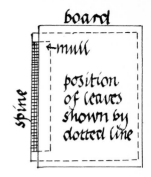

Fig. 50

b Quick Method

Use rubber paste, Copydex or other quick-drying adhesive, so that no drying under pressure is needed, and work can proceed without delay. To preserve brushes, all quick-drying and rubber adhesives should be applied with a thin strip of card which can be thrown away after use.

The book will now look as Fig. 50.

STEP 12: Cut a piece of book-cloth which is 40 mm longer than the length of the boards, and as wide as half the width of the book plus 20 mm. It will thus be large enough to cover one quarter of the width of the book on both sides, plus 10 mm to wrap round the spine, plus another 10 mm so that the cover papers will subsequently be able to overlap the linen by about 5 mm.

Fig. 51

STEP 13: Fold the linen in half lengthways and draw a pencil line down the crease. Draw another line 20 mm from the top edge (Fig. 51).

STEP 14: Paste the linen, and lay it flat on clean waste paper. Place the closed book on it with the spine almost touching the middle line, and the head level with the top line. There will be a 20 mm flap at each end (Fig. 52).

Holding the book in place with one hand, use the free hand under the top two sheets of waste paper to wrap the linen over the spine and smoothly on to the top board. Rub down well.

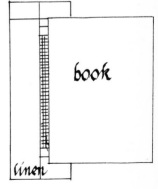

Fig. 52

Stand the book up, ignoring what happens to the linen at the tail, open the cover boards and wrap the 20 mm flap at the head over the boards, tucking it well down between the boards and the leaves. You will now appreciate why the outside sewing holes must not be nearer than 25 mm to the head and tail of the leaves.

Reverse the book and repeat the process at the tail end. This step could be carried out with the book lying open and flat on the table, but if this is done, care must be taken not to drag the binding tight across the spine, or the book will not open and close easily, and the leaves will protrude past the fore-edges of the boards.

There will be a lumpy fullness in the binding at the head and tail of the spine, which must be neatly smoothed and rounded with a pencil or large knitting needle. There is not sufficient room to use the fingers (see Figs. 53 and 54).

Using a bone folder, and with the book closed, gently but firmly press the linen against the edge of the boards along the hinge (A–B in Fig. 55) to give a neat appearance and keep the binding strong.

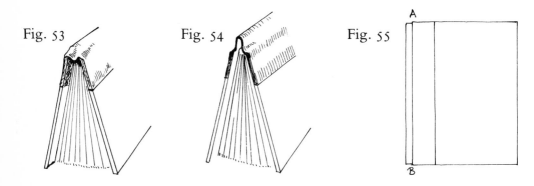

Fig. 53   Fig. 54   Fig. 55

STEP 15 : It is now advisable to allow the book to dry under pressure for about 45 minutes before measuring, cutting and attaching the cover papers, as described on pages 29–33. It is possible to proceed with the work without this 45-minute delay, providing care is taken to leave undisturbed the still–damp edges of the linen, or not to tear it when marking the boards for the position of the cover papers. Children usually want 'to get on with it'!

STEP 16: IMMEDIATELY the cover papers are attached, the endpapers must be stuck to the inside of the boards to act as lining papers. This is necessary to correct the tendency for the boards to warp, as they will begin to do as soon as the cover papers are in place.

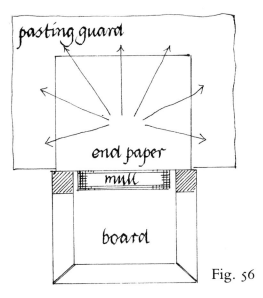

Fig. 56

The technique is to paste the side of the endpaper which is next to the board, using pasting guards and brushing in the direction shown by the arrows in Fig. 56. The pasting guard will protect the rest of the leaves from the paste. After pasting, remove the guard and close the book. The endpaper will adhere to the board. Open the book again, place a sheet of clean waste paper over the endpaper and carefully rub down, paying particular attention to the area adjacent to the sewn part of the book (i.e. the area around the mull) to avoid creasing.

Repeat the process at the other end of the book.

STEP 17: Allow to dry under light pressure.

Zig-Zag Endpapers

A single-section book of more than about a dozen leaves often refuses to lie flat when open. This is because the endpapers, being pasted firmly to the inside of the boards, are unable to adjust to the thickness of the leaves and the hinge-action of the covers. It is not often that primary school children need to make so thick a book, for twenty or so sides of A4 paper presents a formidable challenge to even the most prolific of them. But knowing how to construct endpapers that will expand to accommodate the tensions of the opening boards is a valuable refinement of a bookbinder's skills, and will enable him to produce a better book of any thickness.

Take three pieces of paper, of a quality suitable for endpapers and of a colour to suit the book being made, each of which is the same size as a double leaf. Fold each piece in half accurately and sharply and mark a faint pencil line along the length of each, 3 mm from the folded edge.

Fig. 57 (1–7)

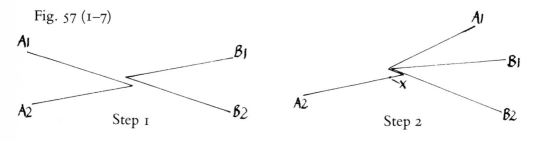

Step 1   Step 2

STEP 1: Using a quick-drying glue join two of the folded sheets, A and B, together along the pencil line, and faintly mark the leaves A1, A2, B1, B2.

STEP 2: Fold A1 over at the fold in Sheet B using a straight-edge to achieve a firm crease.

STEP 3: Crease A2 at x and fold as shown in diagram.

STEP 4: Tear off A1.

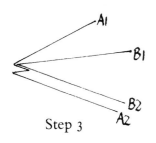

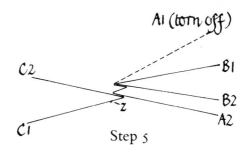

Step 3 — Step 5

STEP 5: Glue sheet C along pencil line as in diagram, and mark the leaves C1 and C2 as shown.

STEP 6: Crease and fold C1 at z and cut off C2 as shown in the diagram.

STEP 7: The double zig-zag thus made provides endpapers B1 and C1, which will be pasted to the boards, and flyleaves A2 and B2 between which the folded leaves are placed before stitching.

From this point the work proceeds from Step 3 on page 43.

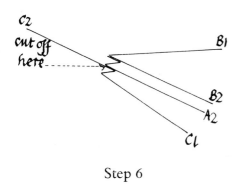

Step 6

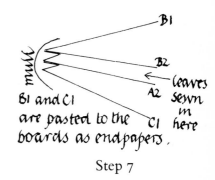

Step 7

CHAPTER II

Towards Craftsmanship – 4

If the children are going to learn to be self-reliant it is essential that all necessary tools, equipment and materials are easily accessible and readily available. This is especially so in the case of clean waste paper which the children will use in prodigious quantities if they are trained to discard all soiled and sticky paper as quickly as possible. Newspaper should be prepared for use by slitting the fold with a large dinner knife or thin steel rule, and then placed in a tidy pile ready for use. Such periodicals as the Radio Times with the staples removed and slit up the back, are an ideal size on which to stand a paste or paint pot. There should be available, at all times, several piles of different sizes, half and quarter sheets of newspapers and periodicals.

Folded pages, where the top sheet can be removed only by tearing, are useless. And so is the system of covering the whole working surface with overlapping sheets of paper. Overlapping sheets cannot be quickly and easily removed and replaced, so sooner or later, and usually almost immediately, the children put their work down on a sticky or dirty patch and ruin it. Paste and paint can soon transfer to the hands and the results can be quite disastrous for the children and their work.

The ONLY satisfactory way to work is on a pile or pad of single sheets, the size of which must be bigger than the work in hand but not necessarily covering the whole work area. It is then so easy for a partner to remove the top sheet as soon as it is soiled, whereupon the work can be immediately replaced on the next clean sheet. (See pages 30 and 31.)

In making books, work should always progress at the quickest possible pace, but without haste. Hurried work gives poor results – improperly pasted papers do not stick at the edges – but the sooner a piece of properly pasted paper is placed in its intended position, the better, for it will have less time to curl up or dry out. Cloth, especially, tends to curl up quickly after pasting, so here a partner can hold a corner in place.

One way in which work can be speeded up without impairing efficiency is by supplying the children with the biggest tools that they can handle. A line on a piece of paper can be more easily and accurately followed with long-bladed scissors than with nail scissors. Paste brushes should never be less than 25 mm wide, and 40 mm is even better. A few brushes of 50 or 60 mm are very useful to have. Some very tiny job of pasting might be successfully accomplished with a small brush, but nothing is more awkward and uncraftsmanlike than trying to paste a large piece of paper with a size 6 paint brush.

Brushes are expensive, but they should last a long time if washed with soap and water immediately after use, carefully rinsed, and dried on a piece of clean rag and then left to dry thoroughly in a warm place, before being replaced in their proper container or drawer.

Training children to 'clear up', and providing the facilities that they may do so, needs thought and planning by the teacher. One waste paper bin per classroom is quite inadequate. Some empty boxes are useful so that children discarding soiled waste paper have something at hand into which it may be dropped immediately.

It is a good habit to clear up as soon as one step is completed, before the next step is tackled. For example, having finished making a cover paper, immediately put away the wax crayons, paints or whatever has been used, wash and dry all used brushes and check that all soiled waste paper has been put in the rubbish box, before starting to fold and sew the leaves. It cannot be stressed too strongly that this kind of training is essential for a happy and disciplined environment.

Mistakes in Marking Out, Measuring and Cutting
It is not uncommon for children to make mistakes in measuring and marking out. To try to erase mistakes from book-cloth or coloured paper almost always leads to spoiling the surface or creasing and tearing it. The most satisfactory method of making corrections is to re-measure and re-draw using a nicely-sharpened coloured pencil crayon, leaving the original and

wrong pencilled lines and marks as they are. It will then be quite easy to distinguish the correct lines and ignore the wrong ones. All measurements should be lightly made and drawn on the uncoloured side of book linen. If it is ever necessary to draw on the 'right' or 'face' side of materials the markings should be as small and inconspicuous as possible.

If mistakes are made in cutting materials too small, there is no remedy but to start again, so it is well worth remembering the old adage of the carpenter, 'Measure twice and cut once'!

Further Developments of the Single-section Book with Board Covers

It is not always appreciated that ordinary fabric makes a fine binding for children's books, as a change from, and an inexpensive substitute for, commercial book-cloth. It is erroneously believed that cotton fabric will allow the paste to ooze through and so spoil the work. This does not happen in practice, unless the paste is very thin and watery. Of course, the fabric must be carefully chosen; loud, large and garish patterns and colours must be avoided. The ideal cloth is a piece of light-weight cotton which has been tie-dyed or printed by the children themselves. They will have then paid due consideration to colours and patterns, in connection with the general plan and purpose of the whole book.

The exciting possibility now presents itself that the children may make a FULLY BOUND single-section book using cloth they have prepared themselves. This means that instead of a book with a cloth binding on the spine, and paper covers, the book may be bound fully in one operation, spine and covers complete. The project presents no difficulty to anyone who has successfully made the quarter-bound version.

Having prepared the cloth cover, about 20 mm bigger all round than the open book, follow Steps 2–11 described on pages 43–7, and then proceed as follows:

1. Paste the cloth cover and lay out flat on the clean waste paper.
2. Lay the closed book on the right-hand side of the pasted cloth so that there is an equal margin at head, tail and right fore-edge (Fig. 58). As it is difficult to draw lines on the cloth, the eye must be the sole judge in estimating the equality of the margins.
3. Placing the left hand under the top two or three sheets

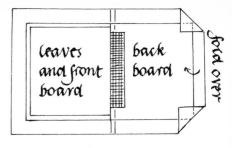

Fig. 58   Fig. 59

of waste, carefully wrap the cloth over the spine and on to the front board. Rub down well. At this stage the pasted margins will probably stick together.

4 Open the book to the back board, separating the stuck margins. Fold in the corners, followed by the fore-edge flap. Rub down. The cloth at the head and tail will be in a wrinkled fold. Ignore it temporarily (Fig. 59).

5 Fold back the leaves and treat the front board similarly.

6 Stand the book up and tuck over the flap at the head.

7 Reverse the book and repeat at the tail.

8 Round off the cloth at the head and tail of the spine (see Figs. 53 and 54).

9 Press binding against the edge of the boards at the spine (Fig. 55, line A–B).

10 Attach endpapers as before (Fig. 56).

11 Allow to dry under pressure.

FORE-EDGE AND CORNER BOUND BOOKS

Another variation of the single-section book with board covers can be made by modifying the quarter-bound version.

Proceed with Steps 1 to 14 described on pages 43–8, until you have a book with the spine bound, but lacking cover papers. Then as the title suggests, the fore-edges of the boards are bound with strips of book–cloth of the same kind used on the spine. Care is needed with the corners because book-cloth is thicker than paper, and a lumpy corner is not attractive. The finished and attached strip of book-cloth should be 2–3 mm more than half the width of the binding on the spine. The cover paper will then consist merely of a strip sufficiently wide just to cover the edges of the binding at the spine and the fore-edge, and long enough to allow flaps of 20 mm at the head and tail (Fig. 60).

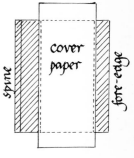

Fig. 60

The endpapers are then pasted down, and the book dried under pressure, as previously described.

The corner-bound version is made by first completing Steps 1–14 as before, and then preparing corner pieces of book-cloth as follows:

1   Make two marks on each of the four unbound corners of the boards which measure, from the corner, a quarter the width of the book plus 2–3 mm, e.g. the measurement for a book 200 mm wide will be 53 mm (Fig. 61).

2   Now mark out and cut the corner pieces of book-cloth as shown in Figs. 62 and 63. This gives an opportunity to use up pieces of cloth that would be too small for most other jobs.

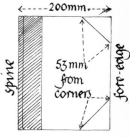

Fig. 61

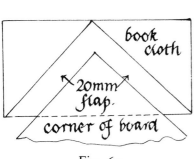

Fig. 62

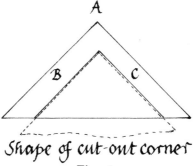

Fig. 63

3   Paste and attach the prepared corner pieces, folding in the apex A (Fig. 63) first before the flaps B and C (ref. to Figs. 28 and 29, page 32). N.B. The corner pieces may be prepared and attached using the 'mitring' method described on page 39. The corner will be less

bulky, but will require very exact workmanship to give a satisfactory result.

4   The cover papers should now be cut to the correct size and shape as follows:

Working on the INSIDE of the cover board, mark six points, shown in Fig. 64 as A, B, J, K, L and M.

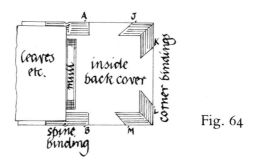

Fig. 64

Marks A and B are those previously described on page 36 for aligning the edge of the cover paper, and shown in Fig. 36 as points C and D. Marks J, K, L, M, are measured from the corners of the board and will be one quarter of the width of the board; i.e. width of board, 200 mm, then distance from corner to J, K, L, M, will be 50 mm.

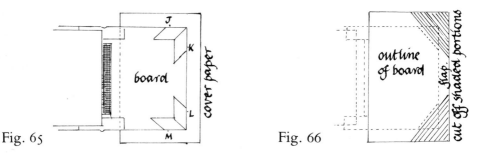

Fig. 65   Fig. 66

5   Cut the cover papers to allow a 20 mm margin or flap at the head, tail and fore-edge. Place the board on the cover paper, draw round the head, tail and fore-edge of the board and mark off the corners (Fig. 65).

Remove the board. Draw lines through the corner markings on the cover paper and cut off these corners (Fig. 66).

6   Attach cover papers, paste down endpapers and dry under pressure.

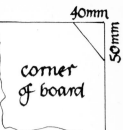

The appearance of a corner-bound (or half-bound) book may be altered, if so desired, by setting the corner-pieces obliquely. This is achieved by altering one of the measurements in each corner, as suggested in Fig. 67. Full-binding, fore-edge and corner binding may of course be applied to the loose-leaf folders previously described. Zig-zag books may also have a cloth instead of a paper cover, or may have the corners bound in cloth. The variations possible, then, with the different kinds of books and bindings means that no child need ever make his 'next' book the same as his 'last' book, if he wants a variation.

Fig. 67

If all pasting is carried out carefully, and with the proper techniques, and the hands kept clean with a piece of rag, there should never be any paste in the wrong place spoiling the work. Sometimes, however, a spot of paste may accidentally stray, with the result that when the finished book is removed from pressure, a piece of the waste paper wrapping is found firmly stuck to it. This can sometimes be removed with a soft eraser, or gently scraped off with a knife, if the unwanted paper is moistened with a fingertip.

Sometimes, when a very special book is being made, it is worth using cheap, plain paper such as kitchen paper, instead of newspaper, for pasting processes.

Children respond very warmly if they know that their work is regarded so highly that the teacher is prepared to let them use kitchen paper for such a purpose. The great advantage of kitchen paper is that it has no printing ink to transfer so easily to working hands, with the danger that black fingerprints may appear in unwanted places. Too much pressure on drying books may also transfer printing ink to the work. So it is always worth considering using kitchen paper at least for separating leaves from covers, and for placing round the outside of books which are about to be dried under pressure. This paper can always be used again after the dampness from the previous use has dried out of it, making the cost quite light. Of course, paper that comes into direct contact with paste and glue is discarded immediately after use, and so must be regarded as expendable. If the use of kitchen paper makes the children more aware of the potential beauty and importance of their work, and raises the standard of their craftsmanship, then the money it costs is well spent.

The skills and techniques so far described are adequate for most children in the Primary or Middle School stage. There is no reason why some children should not pursue the craft in more depth and attempt some form of multi-section binding, but for the majority, the type of work so far described will be sufficient. Anyone who wishes to pursue the craft further for his own satisfaction will find helpful books of instruction in the Bibliography.

ALLIED PROJECTS

CHAPTER 13

Cards, Envelopes, Calendars and Jotters

Attention can now be turned to some other useful projects enjoyed by the children, which can be carried out with the techniques and methods already learnt for making books.

The approach of Christmas offers opportunities for the children to make greetings cards with envelopes, calendars for the new year, and little books and jotters for presents.

GREETINGS CARDS

Cards are most simply made from a piece of folded cartridge paper. This makes a good surface for a carefully written message. The frontal decoration can be applied either direct to the paper, or carried out on a separate piece which is afterwards attached to the cartridge paper base with a few spots of quick-drying adhesive.

The decoration itself can be carried out in so many different ways with so many different media, that it is impossible to explore the possibilities in detail in this book.

There follows a list of suggested activities:

1 A pencil or pen drawing.
2 A small collage.
3 A wax sgraffito.
4 A small watercolour.
5 A lino-print.
6 A screen-print. Small screens can be made from thick strawboard or hardboard, covered with bookbinder's muslin. Stencils of newspaper or kitchen paper are satisfactory. A good printing medium is made from paste mixed with powder colour, applied through the screen with a small piece of sponge. Very simple motifs like Christmas trees or stars give pleasing results.

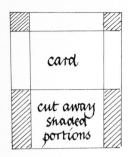

card

cut away
shaded
portions

Fig. 68

Envelopes to fit the cards can be made without a pencil or ruler. The card is placed on a piece of paper (kitchen paper is quite suitable) and the 'network' made by folding. Cutting is carried out along the folds where necessary, and the flaps stuck down. The envelope will be of the same design as that described in Chapter 6 on pages 23–6. If several cards of approximately the same size are made, it is worth cutting a thin cardboard template slightly larger than the biggest card round which the folding is done. This will ensure an easy fit when the cards are inserted. The envelope paper must be cut to size first, of course, allowing dimensions as follows:

Twice the width of the card plus 20 mm one way, by the length of the card plus 40 mm the other way. The extra bits are for the necessary flaps. The diagram of Fig. 68 makes clear the simple process.

CALENDARS

These offer scope for the bringing together of several skills.

A calendar could be made as a simple single-section book, each leaf being devoted to one month of the year, with, for example, a lino-block picture on the top half and the dates on the lower. To save a good deal of repetitive measuring, the framework or grid for a month could be carefully drawn on a piece of thin white card and then inked over fairly thickly to act as a guide which can be traced on each page of the calendar. If this guide is made on a piece of card exactly the same size as the calendar leaves, there will be no difficulty in alignment (Fig. 69).

To save any measuring at all, the guide could be drawn on a piece of squared paper. The only title necessary on a finished calendar would be CALENDAR 19 . . . .

The standard of handwriting on the calendar must be very high (see Chapter 16) and since it is comparatively easy to make a mistake in counting, it is best first to mark out the months very lightly in pencil and then ink over after checking.

Many children like to make a 'one picture' calendar by covering a piece of strawboard with a cover paper and then

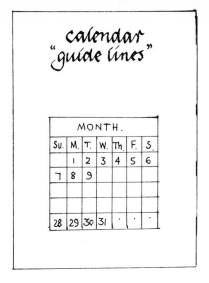

Fig. 69

attaching a picture and a small calendar pad. Two designs are shown in Figs. 70a and 70b.

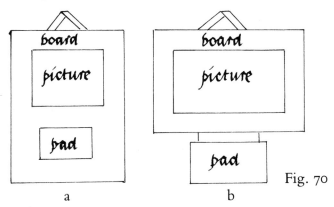

a   b   Fig. 70

Here are the steps for design *a*:

1 Prepare a calendar pad.
2 Prepare a cover paper and suitable picture.
3 Cut board and cover it.
4 Cut lining paper.
5 Attach hanging tape with two blobs of glue on the back of the board 10 mm from the top edge.
6 Attach lining.

7   Attach picture to upper half of front.
8   Dry under pressure.
9   Attach calendar pad with several spots of glue.

Steps for design *b*:
  1–5 as for *a*.
  6   At lower edge of back, attach a small piece of matching book-cloth 25 mm wide and just shorter than the length of the calendar pad (Fig. 71).
  7   Attach lining paper.
  8   Attach picture centrally on front.
  9   Dry under pressure.
  10   Attach calendar pad to the lower edge of the book-cloth tab, leaving a small space between board and pad to allow the pad to be folded back for insertion into an envelope if desired.

Fig. 71

JOTTERS AND SMALL NOTEBOOKS

When about to embark upon an educational visit, children are generally very keen to take with them a small pocket notebook or note pad in which they can draw or make notes about anything that seems to them of importance. Such a little book is often more useful than some of the most carefully prepared questionnaires, which may tend to be too adult-orientated, or which become such a burden that the children stop looking, observing and enjoying, in their anxiety to get the questions answered. But teachers will find that children who are pleased with the neat notebook which they have specially made themselves will do a great deal of spontaneous and purposeful recording, even though some of it may not be quite what the teacher anticipated!

There are many different types of small folders, notebooks and note pads described in some of the books given in the Bibliography, but here are the steps for making a small, simple jotter, which can be modified at will by adding covers or other refinements:

STEP 1: Cut a thin card backing, the size required.

STEP 2: Cut the required number of pages, the same size as the card backing.

STEP 3: 'Tip' the whole lot with paste. This means spreading out the leaves and backing so that their top edges lie about 2 mm apart. Then paste as in Fig. 72.

STEP 4: Knock the lot up square. Cover with clean waste paper and dry under pressure.

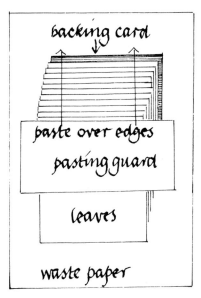

Fig. 72

Binding Single Sheets

The following method can be used for binding the sheets of a calendar pad, or for binding any set of single sheets, providing there is sufficient margin at the sewing edge. This method may be regarded as an alternative to making a loose-leaf folder. The only difference from the orthodox single-section sewn book lays in the sewing itself:

THE METHOD: Knock the single leaves, and endpapers if required, up square. Place a piece of mull round the edge to be bound and secure with a spot of Copydex at each corner. Draw a line down the book 5 mm from the fold of the mull. Along this line mark intervals of about 10 mm (Fig. 73) and pierce with an awl. Insert a holding needle or pin into each mark.

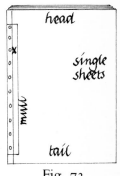

Fig. 73

67

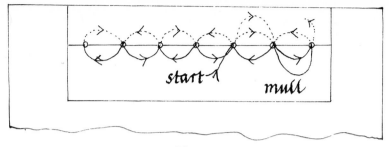

Fig. 74

The main difficulty in this construction is to hold the book still and steady during sewing, so that no trimming is necessary afterwards. Apart from a partner's helping hand, and the use of holding needles or pins, it is useful to have some 'bull-dog' clips to hold the loose leaves steady. As many as are necessary or desirable may be placed on the head, tail and fore-edge.

Start sewing at the hole marked 'X', or thereabouts, going in and out in a simple 'stab' stitch till the last hole is reached, when the sewing is continued back again to the other end and finally back to the start. Make two or three extra stitches over the first stitches done, and pull the sewing tight. The ends of the thread should remain firmly in place, but may be secured completely with a little quick-drying adhesive (Fig. 74). This will avoid having to tie unsightly knots, which would show through and spoil the binding of the finished book.

If the book is to have board covers, the boards should be set close up to the line of sewing. Having been sewn up, the book is then bound in the manner described in Chapter 10.

This method of binding single sheets is, again, one which has been devised by some Oxfordshire teachers when the need for it arose while working with children.

DECORATED COVERS

Examples of printed cover papers: *back, left to right*, rubbing, potato print, grass print, lino print; *front, left to right*, dyed wax rubbing, paste print

CHAPTER 14

Different Cover Paper Techniques

A. WAX RUBBINGS

This method of making cover papers is a firm favourite with children, and demands no special skills. Care and patience are the only two qualities needed.

A textured surface, such as wood with a pronounced grain pattern, the 'rough' side of frosted glass, the side of a wire waste paper basket, a wall, a grating cover, etc., is first brushed clean. A piece of paper is placed over the clean surface and a wax crayon is rubbed on the paper, thus reproducing the texture on the paper.

The finished rubbing is then painted all over with a paper dye, like 'Brusho', or very much diluted Indian ink. The background thus becomes tinted, while the dye 'runs off' the wax which resists it. The finished paper is then allowed to dry naturally and completely, which takes about two hours in a warm atmosphere.

To avoid a 'scribbled' effect, use a piece of crayon about 20 mm long, and use it flat on the paper. Never use the ends as if drawing. Stub ends of crayons, that are too small for other uses, can be saved in a box or tin just for this purpose. A rubbing done with a white crayon or a piece of candle or beeswax is more difficult to see while working, but often gives a striking finished result. A piece of candle used on coloured paper gives the result that the pattern shows the original colour of the paper, while the background is a blend of the colour of the paper and the colour of the dye.

To make sure the dye is of the desired shade it is always a good plan to test it on a piece of spare paper of the sort being used; it is helpful if a partner holds the paper still during the rubbing.

When dyeing the paper, work on sheets of clean newspaper

and take the brush, the largest possible, right over the edges in steady strokes, all in one direction. The brush must be washed in soap and water immediately after use, or it will keep discharging dye every time it is used for weeks afterwards. The top two or three sheets of newspaper, which will be stained, can be discarded after use, and the wet cover paper carried to a convenient place to dry on the next sheet or two of clean, dry newspaper. Children will accomplish the whole task, including the clearing up, in fifteen to twenty minutes.

B. USING COLOURED PASTE

Some cold water paste must first be prepared. Also required will be five small pots of powder colour, black, white, and the three primaries, red, yellow and blue. With the smallest children, the teacher may prefer to add the paint to the paste herself and so make jars of ready-mixed coloured paste, but for the older and more experienced children it is better to keep the colours separate, both from an educational and economical viewpoint. This will become clearer later. The consistency of the paste is important (see Chapter 2, page 7).

1. A Paste Sandwich

For this purpose, the paste must be fairly sloppy (page 8). Two children working together each choose a colour. Paste and paint are mixed for each of the two colours, and each child pastes a piece of paper with the colour of his choice. The two wet sides are then put together in a 'sandwich', laid on newspaper and gently rubbed together. When the two papers are pulled slowly apart, a pattern results naturally, and the two colours are partially blended to give a third. Small children are excited when they realise that by mixing red and yellow, they have made orange. This is true 'discovery for themselves'. The pattern made by this method is affected by the direction in which the papers are pulled apart, and the two papers will each present a slightly different effect from the other, one colour on each being dominant. Plentiful experiment is the best teacher.

2. Paste Combing

A 'comb' is first prepared. It is possible to buy steel combs for

```
┌─────────────────────────┐
│  50 mm .                │
│                         │
│  Cardboard Comb         │
│  (actual size)          │
│                         │
│                         │
│                         │
│                         │
│                         │
│                         │
│                         │
│                         │
│                         │
│                         │
│                         │
│                         │
│  /\  /\  /\  /\  /\ /\  │
└                         ┘   Fig. 75
```

paste combing, but home-made combs are more satisfactory
and quite simple to make from a piece of strong card about
50 mm wide. Simply cut a series of notches along one edge, as in
Fig. 75. The paper is first damped, and coloured paste is rolled
evenly all over it. The comb is then scraped over the paper in
zig-zag, straight or wavy lines, in one direction or both. The
teeth of the comb scrape away most of the paste in their path,
leaving a white pattern behind. This sort of pattern calls for
bold, quick treatment, but because the paper was damped
before using, there will be time to brush out the first effort if
unsatisfactory, and make another attempt before the work dries
out. The children must be shown that it is usually better to carry
the comb right across the paper without pause, so producing an
'all over' effect. Patterns made like a Union Jack may look well
as a unit, but do not look right if the paper is later to be cut in
half to make two separate cover papers.

NOTE: The easiest way to dampen paper is to hold it under a
running tap, or immerse it in a bowl of water. After allowing
the excess water to drain off, it is placed between sheets of clean
blotting paper for a few seconds.

3. Paste Printing

A non-absorbent, smooth flat surface is required for paste printing. A Formica-topped desk or table is admirable.

A dessertspoonful of paste is put directly on the surface. To this is added a saltspoonful of the chosen powder colour, followed by a sprinkling of black, or white, or both. This addition of 'salt and pepper' produces some subtle and sometimes unexpected tints and shades. It turns the raw primary colour into something more interesting. The paste and colour is now mixed up with a brush or rubber roller and then spread out over an area bigger than the piece of paper on which the print will be made.

A pattern is made in the wet coloured paste in one of the following ways:

1   With the roller or brush.
2   With a comb or cardboard strip.
3   With a finger (or two).
4   By placing cut or torn shapes (newspaper will do) on the paste.

The cover paper is then lowered on to the pasted patterned surface, and gently rubbed all over with the TIPS of the fingers. The amount of pressure applied decides the nature of the finished pattern.

Taking a corner of the sheet, peel the paper off with a smooth pull. Lay it aside to dry.

When making cover papers in this manner, it is very necessary to give some thought to the organisation of the worktop. A bowl of water and two cloths, one to be kept dry, are needed to clean the surface and the roller or brush between successive uses, if the next person wants to use a completely different colour. Sometimes, however, some interesting results occur when successive colours are allowed to mingle, instead of being cleaned up each time.

It will soon be discovered that it is necessary to use the roller very lightly to spread the medium, and rather more heavily to make a pattern. Heavier pressure makes the roller slide.

In case of any difficulty in finding a suitable surface, a piece of hardboard, sealed and painted with an oil-based paint to make it waterproof, makes a suitable surface, and one that is transport-able, moreover. Successful results can also be obtained on a piece of Contact, the covering sometimes used on larder shelves, providing it can be pinned down with its backing taut and smooth to make an unwrinkled surface.

In suggestion 4 above, using paper shapes, the shapes on the finished paper will appear white. These shapes can be made clearer and more attractive by carefully outlining the perimeter with a sharp wax crayon of matching colour. It is difficult to do this neatly with a thick, blunt crayon. For a cover paper for a maths book, for example, geometric shapes would be very suitable. And here, there is an opportunity to teach, or reinforce, some mathematical vocabulary.

C. WATER-PROOFING

All cover papers that contain paste or water-based printing ink (see page 86) in their decoration are best waterproofed before use, otherwise the decorative side is liable to become sticky when the back is pasted for attachment to the cover boards. This would make the paper almost impossible to handle, and also spoil the pattern by turning it into a character-less smudge. Furthermore, the waste paper would adhere firmly to it when the book was placed aside to dry under pressure.

Waterproofing is carried out by applying, in small circular movements, any kind of wax polish, with a pad of clean cloth. After a few minutes drying, the paper is polished with another soft cloth. One treatment is sufficient for waterproofing, and it will be noticed that the wax shows right through the paper in places on the back. The patterned side will take on a deeper and richer appearance, and the finished book will have the smell of well-polished furniture and a good, smooth feel.

Some children like to repeat the polishing process several times. Some even want to take their papers home to put in more work on them! If the polishing is done several times, the paper will eventually show quite a high gloss, as though it has been varnished. So the amount of polishing carried out depends on personal taste, plus the ability to persist in a fairly exhausting task!

Some unusual results are sometimes obtained by using coloured polishes – boot polish for example – the colour of which will stain any white parts of the pattern and considerably affect the coloured portions.

However little or much polishing is done, it must be done lightly and cautiously, for it is very easy to catch the edge of the paper with the rag, or to crumple the paper, as is known to happen sometimes when using an eraser. Creases in materials will usually disappear when paste is applied prior to attaching to a board, but it is better to avoid any creasing from the outset.

Printed Covers

PAPER COVERS

A. Printing with Scrap and Natural Materials

Feathers, leaves, corks, pieces of wood or expanded poly-
styrene, string, cotton reels, coarse-woven fabric wrapped
round a blackboard rubber, cardboard tubes and many other
objects all make excellent printing blocks, using powder
colours or water colours as a printing medium. A little paste or
vegetable glue mixed with the colour will help it to adhere
better to a smooth or shiny printing block. In this case,
remember any necessary waterproofing afterwards. It is
necessary only to paint the block with a brush, or to press it on a
pad of plastic foam in a shallow dish, impregnated with colour
(Fig. 76) and then lightly press it on to the paper. With this
informal kind of printing, spacing and layout must be judged
by the eye, and a pleasing arrangement arrived at in this
manner. The consistency of the medium and the quantity to use
are best learnt by letting the children experiment on lots of quite
small pieces of paper, all differing in texture and colour. These
experiments themselves, bound into a book with notes, would
make an excellent reference or sampler book for subsequent use.

Fig. 76

Some of the objects mentioned above would make very
good motifs for a lemon juice discharge print (see page 87).

Cover papers can be made by combining two processes. For
example, on a dyed wax rubbing background, a drawing done
in wax crayon is a worthwhile addition. Or again, a paste-
printed background (showing just the texture of the brush or
roller) would be enhanced by overprinting in a darker colour
with a string and cardboard block. Both these examples have
been taken from work actually carried out by children.

String blocks are very simple to make. Cut a piece of strong
card to the required size, trace on it a simple shape in quick-

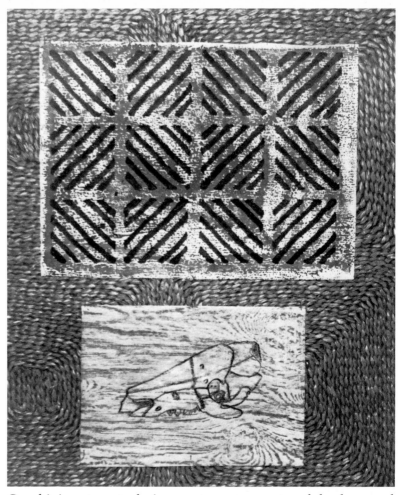

Combining two techniques: *top* paste-textured background overprinted with string block; *below* wax crayon drawing on wax-rubbing background

drying colourless glue and lay a piece of string on the glue shape (Fig. 77).

With any sort of rectangular printing block, it is wise to mark the 'top' on the back, so that the printer will know which way up to place the block on the paper or cloth.

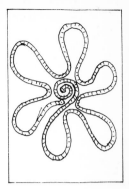

Fig. 77

B. Potato Printing

Potatoes are the best-known natural printing block. The simplest method is to cut the potato in half, paint the cut surface and press it on the paper, leaving behind a coloured print the shape of the cut surface. The next logical step is to cut away a little of the flat surface, which introduces more white into the printed design.

It is with a square-cut potato block that the most fascinating work can be done. The secret of good potato printing lies in the preparation and organisation of the work table, so that it does not become quickly cluttered up.

Work on a pile of single sheets of newspaper. Have the printing medium of watercolour, or waterproof ink on another pad of newspaper. Also required will be a camel or squirrel hair paint brush, about size 8 or 10, and a piece of blotting paper about 100 mm square. A ruler, a kitchen or dinner knife and a 'V' shaped lino cutting tool will complete the equipment. A piece of practice paper is useful, as well as the paper to be printed.

Fig. 78

Cut the potato in half with the large knife, as straight and clean as possible. (One potato will make two blocks.) Blot the cut surface. Using the ruler as a guide, cut the sides from the potato block, making the original cut surface as square as possible (Fig. 78). Blot the cut surfaces. Use the knife or lino tool to cut a simple pattern. The untouched surface will print in colour, while the cut portions will remain white in the print, so do not cut away too much (Fig. 79). Blot the patterned surface and coat with paint or ink. Do not load the brush or the block too heavily. Press the block on the practice paper with a slight rocking movement and remove it at once. Study the result to see if modification to the block is needed.

When satisfied with the block, cut a small notch on the back

Fig. 79

of the block to identify the 'top'. Pack up all the scraps of waste potato in the top one or two sheets of newspaper. Carefully wipe the knife and lino tool, for they will quickly rust with the potato juice, and dry the ruler. Remove the rubbish to the waste box, leaving the clean newspaper as a pad for printing the cover paper proper.

Start printing the cover paper in the top left-hand corner. Line up the top and left-hand edge of the block with the top and left-hand edge of the paper. Subsequently line up the left-hand edge of the block exactly on the right-hand edge of the last print, neither leaving a space nor overlapping. Work straight across the paper, completing each row before starting the next. Re-paint the block for each print, and retain the brush between the first and second fingers while printing. Brushes that are laid down have a nasty habit of rolling about, either spoiling the paper or depositing unwanted blobs of medium on the worktop. Although the block must be repainted for each print, it is not necessary to re-charge the brush each time. Alternatively a pad may be used, as in Fig. 76.

Once started, it is best to finish the complete print in one session. A potato block is difficult to preserve for use on another day, since it begins to shrink fairly rapidly, though it may be wrapped in a damp paper towel and plastic bag and kept for up to about two hours.

When the printing is finished, and laid aside to dry, clean up thoroughly at once, especially if the brush has been used with waterproof ink.

VARIATIONS: Many variations of pattern are possible with the same block, by altering its position on the paper:

1   Alternate rows with the block first the right way up, then with the block reversed through 180°.
2   Alternate prints in the same row.
3   Calling the top of the block 'North', the other sides 'East', 'South' and 'West' respectively, and printing the first row N and E alternately, and the second row W and S alternately. Thus the printing unit becomes four times larger, and each unit is not complete until N, E, S and W are all printed. Some children prefer to

Above, left to right, the unit, straight print, alternate rows reversed 180°, alternate prints reversed 180°; *below, left to right* N.E.S.W. pattern, half-drop, using two colours

do this variation by making the first two prints, N and E, and then immediately moving to the second row to print S and W underneath, thus completing the first unit before returning to the first row to start again with N. Great concentration is needed. It is so easy to place the block in the wrong position.

4 'Half-drop' patterns are made by making the first print normally, but placing the second print so that the top of the block comes halfway down the first.

5 Further variations are possible by combining the half-drop principle with one of the other variations already suggested.

6 Two colour work can be done, either with two blocks printed alternately, or with the same block printing first a 'draughts-board' pattern, and then, having been cleaned, filling the empty squares with the second colour.

Incidentally, games boards for draughts, etc. can be made in the same way as the cover of a loose-leaf folder, printing the lining paper with a square, plain block.

Children working together: lino printing and . . .

cleaning up

82

In any instance where alternate squares are to be left blank, either temporarily or permanently, it will be necessary to mark out the first row very lightly in squares the size of the block.

C. Other Vegetables

Satisfactory blocks can be made from most firm root vegetables, and even from some unlikely ones. Carrot, swede, turnip, have all been used, and also the cut surface of a portion of cabbage. Experimenting in printing with different vegetables and printing media (inks, paints, etc.) is not only exciting – it is essential. Try the effect of white and coloured papers; the effect of white paint on dark paper, and the effect on the finished result of the differences of texture of different vegetables.

Fig. 80

D. Lino-blocks

A lino block, not bigger than 75 mm square, is another excellent printing block. If the craft of lino-block cutting and printing is unfamiliar, see Bibliography. Small offcuts of lino, often only 15 mm square, can be fixed to wood sticks or dowels with a contact adhesive (Fig. 80) and cut and used in the same manner as potato blocks.

E. Marbling

Providing that the colours are carefully chosen, marbling produces some very delicate and interesting designs, and is a process that children enjoy very much. Many children, in fact, would spend long hours at it, using sheet after sheet of paper, if they were allowed to do so! Marbled sheets make excellent cover papers, endpapers and flyleaves. Since it is almost impossible to keep the back of the paper completely clean, it is necessary to make three endpapers instead of two. The three endpapers are placed round the folded leaves in the following manner:

Number 1, next to the leaves with the patterned side facing the leaves.

Number 2, the back (or plain) side facing the back of number 1.

Number 3, as number 1.

When the book has been sewn, the backs of numbers one and

two are pasted together. They must then be allowed to dry under pressure before trimming takes place. Number 3 will be pasted to the board.

When the book is finished, there will be a marbled endpaper lining the board, and a double-thickness flyleaf marbled on both sides.

If preferred, a piece of white paper, or toning coloured paper can be substituted for number 1, so that the book will contain a flyleaf which is marbled on one side and plain on the other.

Before describing the process of marbling, a reminder is necessary that marbling paint, or ink as it is usually called, is oil-based, and therefore all equipment needs turpentine substitute (white spirit) or paraffin as a cleansing agent. A preliminary wipe round the marbling tray with some newspaper before cleaning with a paraffin rag, will mop up the beads of water left when the tray is emptied of water.

STEPS IN THE PROCESS OF MARBLING: A tin marbling tray is filled to a depth of 20 mm with cold water. A teaspoonful of vinegar is added to the water. Children soon become adept at judging the quantities without having to measure it out.

Using an eye dropper, a clean one for each colour, spots of marbling ink are dropped on to the surface where they float. If the spot of colour sinks immediately to the bottom of the tray, it is too thick and must be thinned slightly with paraffin. If the colour spreads at once over the whole surface in a fine film, it is too thin and little can be done about it.

When the desired colours are floating, they may be raked or pushed into a swirling pattern with an awl, a matchstick, the handle of an old paint brush or a lolly-stick. Too much 'stirring' will result in the colours breaking up into a myriad of tiny dots, giving an insipid and characterless pattern. Hold the paper (previously cut to size a little smaller than the tray) with the left-hand edge near the surface, and the right-hand edge several centimetres higher. Place the left-hand edge on the surface and gently push the right-hand edge down to roll the paper completely on to the surface. Alternatively, the paper may be held so that the centre touches the water first, and the ends rolled down simultaneously. If the paper were simply dropped

84

flat on to the surface, air bubbles would be trapped, causing sharply-defined white areas to appear on the finished pattern.

Leave the paper on the surface for about five seconds and then lift it off by two adjacent corners. Lay it on two or three sheets of newspaper and leave it to dry. Some children like to wash the finished pattern under a running tap to remove odd spots of surplus colour, after lifting it from the tray. The tips of the fingers will pick up some colour, so wipe it off at once.

It is now possible to marble another piece of paper on the tray at once, without adding more colour. This second print is a paler reproduction of the first, and many children prefer it to the original.

If a second copy is not required, the surface of the water may be cleansed of the remainder of the colour with a sheet or two of newspaper. The next pattern may then be made, starting from the beginning again by dropping fresh colours on the water.

It is worth experimenting with different coloured papers – light grey, beige, and other pale neutral colours are usually best. Coloured papers altogether alter the tone of the colours and give a different effect.

It is also worth experimenting with ordinary house paint thinned down with paraffin. It is a splendid way to use up odds and ends that would normally be thrown away, or left to dry up in the bottom of the tin. When available, some people use rainwater in the tray, in which case no vinegar is needed.

Ready-to-use colours can be obtained from educational suppliers under the name of Linmarbline Marbling Inks (or Colours). These colours are fairly expensive, for the bottles are only about 1 fluid oz. Some of the colours are rather harsh, so here is another chance to experiment in mixing to produce more subtle shades.

The final clean-up needs to be done as soon as the last marbling is finished, for marbling ink sets hard fairly quickly, and is then much more difficult to remove with a paraffin rag. Usually the sink needs a clean as well, because when the water is tipped away, it carries small quantities of paint with it, which cling eagerly to the sink.

CLOTH COVERS

A. Potato and Lino-block

Fine cotton material makes excellent book-covers. New material must be thoroughly washed and pressed to remove the 'dressing', for it will then be softer, and easier to print.

When printing cloth with a potato block, the best medium is fabric printing ink diluted with turpentine substitute (white spirit) to the consistency of writing ink. This means that one is printing in effect with coloured turpentine. Good printing will sink right into the fabric and show through to the back. A piece of cloth prepared in this way in the morning will be dry and ready to use in the afternoon.

When printing cloth with a lino-block, fabric printing ink should be used, this time undiluted and sticky. It will take at least 24 hours to dry, perhaps longer.

Extra supervision is needed when cleaning up after using fabric printing ink, for it is oil-based, and is not soluble in water. Turpentine substitute on a rag must be used to clean every piece of equipment used, and a clean piece of dry rag for the final wipe. Brushes must be first well rinsed in turpentine substitute, and then washed with soap and water. Spots on the hands may be removed with a turps substitute rag, and then thoroughly washed. All rags used for cleaning should be wrapped in newspaper and put in an outside dustbin with a close-fitting lid, for turpentine substitute is highly inflammable.

Caution should be exercised if the medium known as 'Lino-Printing Water Colour' is used. It has the great advantage of being soluble in water and so cleaning up is easy, but it has been known to take a very long time to dry when used on cloth, sometimes even a matter of weeks; and when used on paper for a book cover it has been known to turn sticky when the paper is pasted. When an unfamiliar medium is used, it behoves the user to read the manufacturer's instructions very carefully, and test it on a small sample piece first.

B. Tie-dye and Batik

The techniques of tie-dyeing and simple batik work are fairly well-known today, but if these crafts are unfamiliar, helpful books will be found in the Bibliography. Such a patterned cloth looks well as a book cover, if the design is on such a scale as suits the scale of the book.

With any sort of dyeing, avoid immersing the hands in the liquid. Dye is difficult to remove from hands, and parents sometimes object to their children changing colour while at school. Always use a stick or an old ruler to push the cloth in, to move it about or to remove it to the sink.

C. Discharge Printing

The 'lemon-juice discharge' method of printing, though simple, makes a first-class cover, and is carried out as follows:

1. Dye a suitably-sized piece of cloth in a solution of permanganate of potash (Condy's Fluid). This is cheap and easily available. The cloth is purple when taken from the dye-bath, but turns brown on drying. Wash, dry and press the dyed cloth.

2. Print the dyed cloth in one of the ways just described. A potato block is excellent. Use lemon juice as the printing medium. Paint the block sparingly, or use a pad as in Fig. 76, and remove it from the cloth fairly quickly after each print.

3. The lemon juice will bleach the colour from the cloth, leaving a white pattern on the brown background. The edges of the pattern will appear quite fluffy and soft. This adds to the effect.

THE BOOK'S CONTENTS

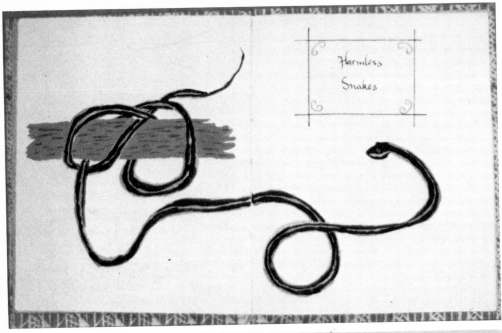

Examples of
title pages

CHAPTER 16

Page Layout, Handwriting and Titles

The importance in the education of children of developing clear, pleasant, workmanlike handwriting is often overlooked or, more sadly, not recognised. Yet it has been the experience of many teachers that the standard of the children's 'written English' improves with growing skill in handwriting, especially when children have a book of their own making into which they can put their written work.

'Handwriting is caught, not taught' has been the maxim of some educationalists for some years. It is true that good models are essential, and it is of paramount importance that the teacher should always set a good example even in writing a simple list or notice for display. But careful teaching and regular short practices are still necessary, for as long as the children have need; that is, until they have acquired good habits especially in forming letters, and have sufficient skill to write fluently and without strain. It is also important that the children should be provided with the best writing tools and materials that the school can afford. Powdery ink, scratchy pens and cheap ball-point pens simply do not bring a satisfactory response from the children, neither do exercise books made of inferior-quality paper.

In Oxfordshire, as in many other places, a simple non-fussy cursive italic hand is favoured, and many excellent books and work cards are available on this subject (see Bibliography).

The italic hand has many advantages. It is easy to learn and teach. It is smooth and speedy when the hand is skilled. It is written with a stiff chisel-edged pen, which is a copy of man's original natural choice for recording his thoughts in pen and ink, a quill or reed cut to shape for writing. This shape gives, quite automatically, the thick and thin strokes, which dominate the character of beautiful handwriting. All that is necessary is to hold the pen at the correct angle. Specially-cut nibs are available for left-handers whose needs have often been ignored.

The italic hand follows easily and naturally from the bold, clear roman print script taught in many Infant departments. Basically, this early script has merely to be compressed slightly and slanted a little to the right. Joining the letters then follows naturally, and no strange new shapes have to be learnt, as in such styles as Civil Service Cursive, which was originally designed for engraving on copper plates, not for writing with pen and ink.

Children love to draw patterns with broad pens and to experiment with quills and reeds. They should be allowed to do so.

What a splendid instrument for drawing is the present almost universal writing tool, the ball-point pen, but what spidery and ill-shaped handwriting it can produce! How convenient it is – no messy ink bottles. But how dull and flat, and what bad effects it has on young children's handwriting, encouraging as it does incorrect habits which are so difficult to overcome afterwards. What a difference there is between a common-place exercise book filled with Biro scribble, and a beautiful and individual hand-made book filled with well-laid-out pages of careful italic handwriting.

Handwriting is a craft in its own right. Children are frowned upon for slip-shod or rough speech, but slip-shod and rough handwriting is accepted. Yet both are our tools of communication. Not every child is physically capable of writing beautifully yet everyone is capable of workmanlike and legible penmanship. We have, sadly, reached a stage today where some of us are obliged to have our names typewritten under our signature, because our handwriting is illegible. Most official forms demand 'BLOCK CAPITALS PLEASE' because of the danger of illegibility and misunderstanding.

So much endeavour, so much thought and endurance were put into man's long struggle to achieve written communication, and so much that is beautiful was achieved by writing masters and craftsmen of the past, that it must be an insult to our forbears to ill-treat what they have taught us, and to think that handwriting no longer matters. Yes, we may adapt to present-day needs, but never abuse or bastardize our heritage.

In connection with children making books, it is imperative that the contents be attractive, and worthy of the skills and care needed for its manufacture. A good italic hand is right for a hand-made book. No special lettering needs to be learnt. Of course, for titles and illuminated initial letters, extra care will be taken in writing them, but the already familiar shapes of the italic alphabet are adequate.

The most pleasing impression comes from the pattern formed by black ink upon white paper, and it is rare that we need resort to coloured paper and inks. The occasional use of red or blue ink can sometimes enhance a page but usually black and white are sufficient.

Just as important as the handwriting itself is the way in which the page as a whole is laid out.

SPACING: The space between words should not exceed the width of the letter o, and the spacing between lines should be just sufficient to accommodate the ascenders and descenders (Fig. 81).

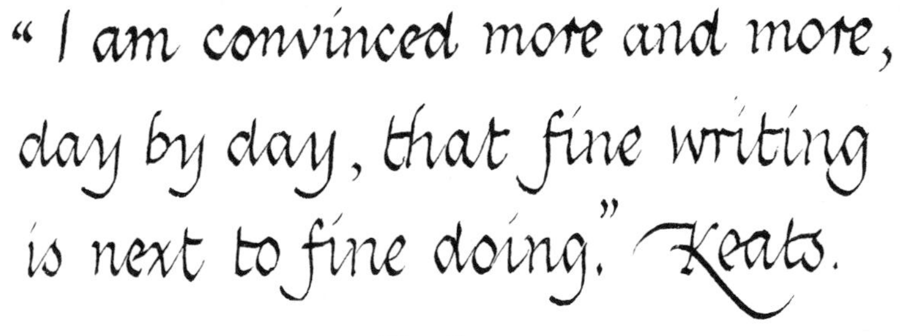

" I am convinced more and more, day by day, that fine writing is next to fine doing." Keats.

Fig. 81

MARGINS: The margins are part of the pattern and are therefore as important as the writing and illustration. The diagram (Fig. 82b) shows proportions which children easily remember, for both single sheets and double. It will be seen that the lower margin is twice as wide as the sides and top.

Elijah
and the ravens

Examples of
finished pages:

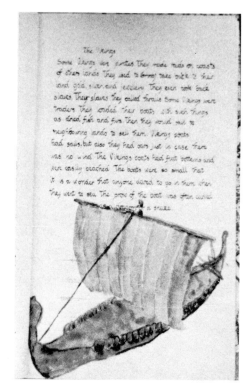

The Vikings

Some children like to pencil the position of the margins before starting to write. The use of a sheet of guide lines underneath the page to keep the lines of writing straight and properly spaced, is a great help. Some children are able to judge the margins by eye.

If a teacher prefers a quick method of marking margins without measuring, it is simple to prepare some strips of card of the required size which can be placed on the edge of the writing page and the margins pencilled in. It is also possible to mark the margins on the guide line sheets. If guide line cards are home-made, rather than printed, they must be ruled quite heavily in ink. Pencil, or pencil crayon lines, though visible through the writing paper, will act rather like carbon paper and spoil the back of the writing paper.

Fig. 82a

Children enjoy decorating their pages with a border of simple pen-drawn patterns, examples of which are shown in Fig. 82a. In this case, the margins are marked out lightly in pencil, then a second line is drawn about 5 mm away on the inside. The pattern is drawn between this double ruling. The pencil lines are erased when the ink is quite dry, and waiting until the next day avoids any danger of smudging. Children show great ingenuity in finishing the corners where the patterns meet, and in spacing the strokes of the pattern so that it is even, regular, and finishes in the right place.

Even if the handwriting is not of the most beautiful, or not of the purest shapes, the finished page will look attractive and ship-shape, providing that sufficient care has been taken in the general layout and spacing.

One's attitude of mind is important as regards handwriting. Good handwriting should be regarded as the everyday norm, not as something special, to be reserved for an Art lesson.

It is a sound plan to use capital (or upper case) letters as a means of emphasis. Titles also look well written in capitals. Underlining can be very ugly and is not found in printed books. Many lessons in layout can be learnt from a well-printed book.

After the flyleaf or leaves, the first 'working' page in a book should be reserved as a title page. Again, well-printed books can be studied as examples of good layout. Much valuable discussion and planning can result from the designing of a title page. However simple the title page may eventually turn out to be, the aim should be symmetry and clarity. It should certainly contain the book's title and the maker's name. Nothing need be written on the back of the title page, except perhaps the name of the class and school, and the date of commencement. A list of contents might be suitable, either on the back of the title page, or perhaps on the next. Some children like to decorate the title page with pen-drawn patterns, drawings, paintings, etchings, or lino prints.

Many well-made books have been spoilt by allowing children to write, sometimes hastily, directly on to the front cover. It is perhaps better to confine all titles to the title page, but if it is decided to write on the cover then a very carefully made label is necessary. The paper for this must be chosen to blend with the binding. The label must be ruled out and carefully lettered, and trimmed to the right size when completed. The position in which it is to be put on the cover must receive due consideration, before it is stuck down.

Careful attention to title pages and layout and all the planning and discussion involved between children and teacher is of the utmost value and more important than the skill of the creator. Providing the children are encouraged to give one hundred per cent effort, the making of the book is as important as the finished product.

CHAPTER 17

Towards Craftsmanship – 5

A. The Beginner

In order to learn, and become reasonably competent at an unfamiliar craft, nothing, of course, can compare with personal tuition, but reading and experience are the next best things.

Having chosen a suitable book of instruction, first read it thoroughly from cover to cover to gain a general idea of the craft and the philosophy behind it. Then read it again, more slowly, carrying out the instructions to the letter, and disregarding any short cuts that may occur to one, since these usually lead to disaster. Carrying out the exercises oneself leads to an appreciation of any difficulties which the children might encounter later, and it also gives one an idea of how much material it will be necessary to prepare for the children.

It is wise to keep carefully one's early efforts. Most people reach a stage in a very short time when they become quite pleased with themselves, almost complacent. When more experience has been gained, the sight of these early efforts has a salutary chastening effect. When we can view our own work with a critical eye, and see faults that had previously escaped our notice, then we are beginning to appreciate the craft, and respect its disciplines.

There are very few young children who do not eagerly assimilate the actual techniques of most crafts. What is surprising is how soon they develop this faculty of self-criticism, often being dissatisfied with work that the teacher would accept. This is very noticeable when they are writing pages for their own books. A small mistake in a pen-drawn pattern which they consider spoils its rhythm, is sometimes enough to make them want to start again on a fresh sheet of paper. Sometimes they are willing to accept with the teacher's help the erasure of a tiny blot or a small spelling mistake, but usually only the 'best' is good enough for their 'best' book.

B. Proportions

In the foregoing descriptions and instructions for making books, certain sizes have been given as examples, but of course a book may be made of any size desired.

It is necessary, though, to observe certain proportions. A square book would seldom 'look right'. A reliable guide is the standard size of paper. From sheets of size A1 may be made books of size A2, A3 or A4 by folding. A nicely-proportioned book from the bookshelf could be measured to ascertain a suitable size. A well-proportioned book will look right whether the longer or shorter side is used as the spine.

Children often prefer to construct a loose-leaf folder with one of the short sides at the back. Then when making the pages, they sometimes prefer to make double columns, as this looks rather better than a solid block of writing (Fig. 82b).

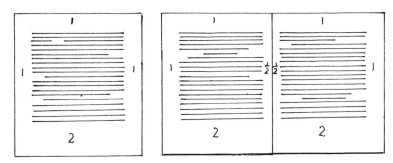

Fig. 82b

C. Occasions for Making Books

Books which the children make themselves have so many uses. They can be filled with written work of all descriptions, and covering all areas of study. A book to hold photographs of a project makes a permanent record. Books of samples are interesting to make, and absorbing for other children to study. Here are a few suggestions for books of samples and recipes:

1 Tie-dyeing – with written instructions.
2 Pottery Record Book – drawings of articles made and instructions.
3 A Book of Lettering and Writing Patterns.

98

4   A Book of Cover Papers – with instructions.
5   A Book of Paintings. Imagine a book, the leaves of which are made of paper which the children have made themselves. Paper-making is within the capabilities of young children.
6   A Book of Lettering done entirely with reeds, quills and home-made ink.
7   Books made to accompany, for example, a piece of handwoven fabric, and describing its manufacture.
8   A Cookery Recipe Book.
9   A Recipe Book for making Vegetable Dyes, containing small samples of dyed wool, preferably hand-spun on a simple home-made spindle.

Some children are encouraged to make 'Topic' or 'Interest' books, and the complaint is sometimes heard that either the pages are all used up before the work is finished, or more often that ideas run out with the book less than half filled. The simple answer to this problem is, in the first case, make volume 2, and in the second to miss a page, calling it a flyleaf, and make a new title page for another subject.

A most useful book for all children to keep is one which may be called a 'general work book', 'best work book', or some other such non-specific title. In it, children can put work of their own selection from their notebook or exercise book, or perhaps a favourite poem. Pages for such a book should be made after the original work has been discussed with the teacher, and the mechanical difficulties of spelling and punctuation, etc. have been sorted out. The 'best page' can then be made with full concentration on producing a beautiful piece of work. This makes very purposeful handwriting practice, better than simply copying a model. The inclusion of a pen-drawn border or an illustration will enhance the work and make it an object of pride and endeavour. The difference in standard between the work and attitudes of a child who has a collection of his own best work in his own best book, and a child who has nothing but a rather sad exercise book is quite startling, and bears no relationship to so-called intelligence.

D. *Teaching new techniques*

Experience would indicate that the best way to teach a new technique, like marbling for example, is to demonstrate to the whole group or class of children while at the same time explaining. It will be found that when individual children then subsequently try it for themselves, there will be a group of interested spectators who want to watch. The teacher, of course, will be one of these. Lively discussion will take place; advice will be freely given, and opinions on the merits, or otherwise, of the artists will be unambiguously expressed. All this can be of immense value, as long as everyone clearly understands that no-one interferes physically with the experimentation. Such situations often encourage the inarticulate to express themselves unselfconsciously, as their interest overwhelms their usual reticence.

E. *Cutting and Storing Bookcraft Materials*

Undoubtedly the best method of cutting bookcraft materials accurately and cleanly, is with a sharp knife and straight-edge. Children who have learnt this skill find the clean crisp edges very satisfying. Thick materials present problems, because some children have difficulty in sustaining sufficient pressure on the straight-edge to keep it steady while the cutting is completed. It is usually the teacher's job therefore to cut the strawboard, and the card cutter is the most convenient tool for this task.

It is possible to buy strawboard in packets ready cut in standard sizes. The strawboard which is designated as '454 g' is the most suitable general purpose material to have in stock. If it is bought in large sheets, the most economical way to buy it, some difficulty may be experienced in holding the sheet quite still during cutting. It tends to slide as the card cutter is used. It is therefore advisable to cut oversize in the first place. If for example some pieces size 250 × 210 mm are required, first cut them 255 × 215. It is then easy to trim the excess from the boards, ensuring accuracy, because the strawboard will not slip if a small margin only is being trimmed off. A pair of large and heavy bookbinder's shears is a very useful tool for the initial cutting of a large sheet.

Children who are going to cut their own materials from large sheets must be taught to cut economically. If left to their own devices the children will soon reduce the stock of the whole class to a pile of large sheets of paper each with a hole in the middle. They must be taught always to cut from the edge of the sheet. If the need is for a rectangular shape, only two cuts need to be made, not four. The conservation of, and respect for, all materials is even more necessary now, in these days of dwindling natural resources and high prices.

It is a good rule to cut an even strip of the desired width, right across the width of the material, and then to cut the strip to the desired length (Fig. 83).

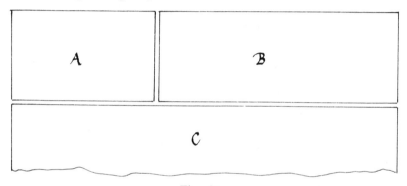

Fig. 83

A is the piece of material needed, B and C the spare pieces. It is easier to store B and C as separate pieces than if B were attached to C. Sooner or later, B will be crumpled accidentally or be torn and so wasted. It is well worth having a separate box or drawer in which the smaller pieces of spare materials can be stored. But this must be known as the 'SPARE' drawer, and never referred to as the 'scrap' drawer.

Another important aspect of the storing of materials and equipment is the availability of it to the children. Children who are making books and know exactly what they are doing and what they need, are going to become very frustrated if they must wait for the teacher to supply each need. Also, a busy teacher with a large class has no time to 'wait upon' a few individuals, so there will be strained feelings all round! There are many excellent pieces of classroom storage furniture on the market, mostly, alas, rather expensive, which contain easily accessible drawers and shelves, and usually with a useful working surface top. Children soon learn which drawer or shelf contains which tools or materials, especially if the drawers and shelves are clearly marked, with well-lettered labels.

The teacher's role is to see that everything used is cleaned and put back in the right place, so that everyone knows where to find what he or she wants at any time. There are some suggestions in Chapter 18 for some home-made or improvised storage equipment.

If, however, there is no suitable storage equipment at all which is easily accessible to the children, then the teacher will have to place the necessary materials and equipment neatly on a table, or a couple of spare desks, first thing in the morning before the children arrive. There are often some habitually early children who might be trained to do this, and also to help pack away at the end of the day. Even the window sills may be brought into use as daily areas for holding tools and materials. Well-trained children who know that much is expected of their common sense and reliability may even be allowed access to the store cupboard. Mutual trust and respect between children and teacher is essential if work by individuals is going to be efficient and smooth, and this mutual trust and respect is attained only when purposes are clear, interest is dominant and good habits are strongly established.

ECONOMY MEASURES

A home-made trimming press in front of a commercial trimming press

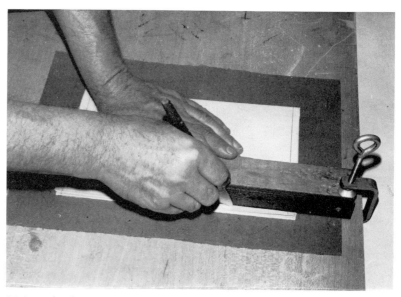

Using the home-made trimming press

CHAPTER 18

Home-made Materials and Equipment

For reasons of economy and to conserve rapidly dwindling world resources it is often necessary to use materials at hand in making books, or in making the tools needed in their construction. The following ideas have all been used successfully, but the list is by no means exhaustive. Ingenuity, and resourcefulness, are characteristics of craftsmen through the ages, and must be encouraged in ourselves and in our children.

A. Materials
Empty boxes and packets when opened out provide sheets of cardboard which, if not suitable for book boards, are useful as cutting boards.

Pieces of cotton or linen sheeting, when stuck on paper with non-synthetic adhesive, can be used as book linen.

Plain flour will make adequate paste when mixed with water, and boiled.

The plain side of wallpaper may be utilised.

B. Equipment
Some skill in carpentry is required in making the following equipment, but no-one need feel daunted. If necessary, the help of a colleague, or a secondary school woodwork specialist could be enlisted. Some Teachers Centres provide the necessary workshop facilities.

Timber merchants will cut materials to size for a small extra cost, and most have a bin of offcuts that often contains pieces of adequate size for the job in hand.

I. TRIMMING PRESS:
Materials: Small drawing board, or similar, approximately 375 mm × 600 mm.

Steel straight-edge 450 mm.

Wood 50 mm × 25 mm × 450 mm.

4 steel countersunk screws, size 6, 20 mm.

4 small rubber buffer feet.

2 cramps 50 mm.

Medium glasspaper.

Assembly: Screw buffers to base of board, approximately 25 mm in from corners.

Drill four 3 mm holes in straight-edge, equally spaced and with outside holes 25 mm in from end. Countersink.

Screw straight-edge to 50 mm × 25 mm wood, allowing bevelled edge to overlap, using the size 6 screws (Fig. 84).

Smooth all edges with glasspaper.

The G-cramps, set upside down, are used to hold the straight-edge in any position across the board.

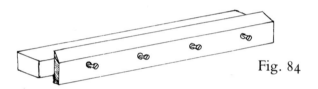

Fig. 84

2. WORKING TOP: (Fig. 85)

Materials: 4 50 mm × 25 mm wood (for lengths see 'Assembly'). $\frac{1}{8}$" hardboard, $\frac{3}{4}$" panel pins, $1\frac{1}{2}$" oval nails. PVA woodworkers glue.

Assembly: Nail four lengths of wood in a rectangular frame to fit over two desks put together.

Glue and pin the hardboard to this frame, smooth side down.

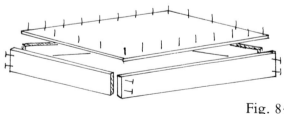

Fig. 85

Well paint inside, so that the working top used upside down will make a good surface for paste printing (Chapter 14, page 74), the frame preventing paste and paint escaping on to the floor.

3. TABLE/CUPBOARD:
Fill in three sides of an old table or wooden desk with hardboard and a useful storage space is made. Battens glued and screwed to the sides and back on the inside will support shelves of blockboard. The top well painted, or covered in Formica or Contact, becomes an easily cleaned working surface.

An old chest of drawers can be similarly converted.

A light glasspapering, followed by coats of clear polyurethane varnish, will improve all wooden items.

4. CONTAINER BOXES:
a Tidy boxes of strong cardboard, available from educational suppliers, are useful to hold small items, like scissors, tins of needles, etc.
b Empty biscuit or similar tins make useful containers. Clean jam jars, with labels removed, hold pencils, brushes, etc.
c Plastic containers are light, but can be prevented from tipping over by placing a weight in the bottom.
d Wooden boxes can be made using the method described for the working top. Panel pins and glue are quite strong enough, and the box will be rigid once the base is fitted.
e Plastic or wooden seed trays make useful storage drawers, and may be stacked on a shelf in the converted table.
f A block of wood drilled about 25 mm–50 mm deep will hold pencils, scissors, awls, etc. A dowel pushed into a hole will make a peg on which to stand a reel of bookbinder's thread. To keep the reel from tangling, push a needle into it and wrap the loose end of the thread around it in a figure of eight. To use the thread simply withdraw the needle.

Fig. 86

5. BOOKBINDER'S AWL:

Insert a bookbinder's needle into a wooden handle cut from a dowel or a broom handle and shaped for comfort. If the hole is prepared with a red hot needle held in pliers the needle can be inserted easily. This awl is much more useful than a bought one, for it makes a much smaller hole (Fig. 86).

6. FOLDING TOOL (Fig. 87):

A short steel knitting needle (approximately 125 mm) sawn in half and fitted into a wooden handle, as for the awl above, makes an ideal folding tool in tight places – when mitring corners or when tucking the linen flap between the boards and the leaves (Chapter 10, page 48).

Fig. 87

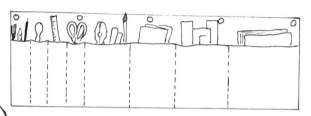

Fig. 88

7. CLOTH STORAGE POCKETS (Fig. 88):

Hessian, or some such strong material, folded lengthwise and stitched vertically at appropriate intervals can provide a strip of pockets to hold various bookbinding items, which can be hung along the wall behind the workbench or table.

8. PRESS:

A flat board, surmounted by a few clean bricks, or a pile of old encyclopaedias, provides sufficient weight for pressing most jobs.

Choosing Materials and Tools

It is sometimes difficult to decide which is the most suitable material to choose for a certain purpose. The notes that follow are intended to help in this respect. The materials mentioned here are all available from the educational suppliers listed on page 113. See also Chapter 18 – Home-made Materials and Equipment.

Pens	For general use, Osmiroid Medium, Straight or Left Hand italic dip nibs. Osmiroid and Platignum Fountain Pens with M.S. or L.H. italic nibs are cheap. Osmiroid may be obtained from Dryad; Platignum from E. J. Arnold. (Addresses on page 113.)
Ink	Quink permanent black.
Cover boards	16 oz (454 g) strawboard is the most useful, with perhaps a few sheets of 24 oz (680 g) for the occasional very large book.
Paper for pages	1 for manuscript books, single sheets or double (fly): plain writing or exercise paper (sometimes called 'Ruling O') 2 for drawing books: cartridge paper (standard quality) or sugar paper 3 for books in which items are to be mounted (photographs, leaves, feathers, cut-out pictures, etc.): sugar paper 4 for books with coloured leaves on which white pages are to be mounted: Oxford Paper, Cambridge Paper (very expensive), Cover Paper, thick sugar or pastel paper.

Paper for marbling, wax rubbings, potato and other prints, pencil drawings	cartridge paper (standard quality).
Paper for flyleaves and endpapers	cartridge paper for white; for coloured, as in no. 4 above.
Book-cloth or linen	There are many different sorts and colours listed in catalogues, but it pays to buy the best quality (e.g. Sundour, Buckram or Clarendon Book Cloth). Only very skilful hands can use cheap book cloth because it is very thin. It sags and stretches when pasted and the surface is easily damaged. Book cloth substitutes, such as Linson, are not recommended because they are paper, not cloth.
For making mull	Bookbinder's Muslin. Very cheap. One square metre will make enough mull for many books.
Paste	Cold-water paste powder (see page 7 for preparation).
Glue	Copydex, Bateman's Rubber Paste, Cow Gum, UHU, Clear Bostik, Mountant Paste (smells like marzipan).
Thread for sewing books	Bookbinder's Medium 16's Thread. Linen Carpet Thread also suitable. Button thread is fair, but very thin.
Needles	Bookbinder's needles (they have a suitably sized eye for bookbinder's thread).
Eyelets	By gross, in assorted colours, or brass, to strengthen and neaten holes in loose-leaf folders.
Wax crayons, powder paint	Usually standard materials in most schools.
For potato printing	Waterproof drawing inks and Indian ink.

For dyeing paper	'Brusho' colours – can usually be mixed much more thinly than instructions on packets indicate.
For lino printing	Fabric printing ink or Printing ink.
Paper for *'pencil writing'*	Kitchen paper.
Colours for marbling	Linmarbline marbling colours.

TOOLS:

Apart from the usual school equipment, scissors, paint brushes, pencils, rulers, crayon pencils, etc. the following tools are useful:

1. Large paint brushes, 25 mm, 50 mm and 75 mm for pasting papers.
2. Marbling tray about 300 mm × 450 mm. This is like a roasting tin, but has square corners and is about 25 mm deep.
3. Two or three rubber covered rollers 100 mm wide for spreading paste or printing ink.
4. Some large scissors, at least 150 mm blades.
5. A pair of bookbinder's large shears.
6. Some knives – 'Card' knives are very suitable, with an oilstone and oil for sharpening.
7. One or two straight-edges. These are of heavy steel. A useful length is 450 mm.
8. A few steel rules, suitably graduated in mm.
9. One or two bookbinder's awls.
10. A hammer and single-hole punch (3 mm).
11. An eyelet tool.
12. A pair of punch pliers for making neat holes in leaves for loose-leaf folders.
13. A card cutter with a blade of about 330 mm.
14. A carpenter's or bookbinder's try-square, for marking out a sewn book ready for trimming.

Bibliography

The following list is by no means exhaustive, but every book listed is most helpful and informative.

MAKING BOOKS:

Bookcrafts for Juniors	A. F. Collins	Dryad Press
Bookcrafts for Senior Pupils	A. F. Collins	Dryad Press
Hand Bookbinding	Aldren A. Watson	Bell Publishing Co. Inc. N.Y.

HANDWRITING:

The Dryad Writing Cards	Alfred Fairbank	Dryad Press
A Manual of Handwriting	Alfred Fairbank	Dryad Press
Cursive Handwriting	Philip Burgoyne	Dryad Press
From Scribble to Script:	Peter Rudland	Out of print, but
Sweet Roman Hand	Wilfred Blunt	possibly available from Public Library

PRINTING AND DYEING:

Children's Work in Block Printing	Robin Tanner	Dryad Press
Dyed and Printed Fabrics	June Hobson	Dryad Press
Simple Screen Printing	Anthony Kinsey	Dryad Press

Dryad Leaflets (listed in Dryad catalogue)

Suppliers of Tools and Materials

The two main suppliers are:
Messrs Dryad Ltd.,
P.O. Box 38,
Northgates,
Leicester, LE1 9BU.
Tel: (0533) 50405.

Messrs. E. J. Arnold & Son Ltd.,
12 Butterley Street,
Leeds, LS10 1AX.
Tel: (0532) 442944.

Catalogues may be obtained on request, and special educational terms may be available. Lists of craft publications may also be obtained.

Metric and Imperial Paper Sizes

Before the traditional and fascinating names are lost to the craft vocabulary, there follows a list of imperial paper sizes. See Chapter 2 for the traditional names of folded sheets.

NAME	SIZE OF FULL SHEET
Foolscap	$17'' \times 13\frac{1}{2}''$
Crown	$20'' \times 15''$
Large Post	$21'' \times 16\frac{1}{2}''$
Demy	$22\frac{1}{2}'' \times 17\frac{1}{2}''$
Royal	$25'' \times 20''$
Imperial	$30'' \times 22''$

Some of these names are preserved, in metric form, by suppliers of book papers, but the only sizes now readily available from stationery suppliers are the A1, A2, A3 series where A2 is half the size of A1 and A3 half the size of A2. A1 is the nearest paper size to Imperial ($30'' \times 22''$) and in fact measures 840×594 mm ($33'' \times 23\frac{1}{2}''$ approx.).

For ready conversions of imperial and metric measurements, the following are useful approximations:

2–3 mm	$\frac{1}{8}''$
5–6	$\frac{1}{4}''$
10	$\frac{1}{2}''$
20	$\frac{3}{4}''$
25	$1''$
50	$2''$
300	$12''$ (1 ft)
330	$13''$
450	$18''$

In the example on page 34, the imperial measurements for Fig. 32 would be:

BOARDS	$10''$	$\times\ 8''$
LINEN No. 1	$9\frac{3}{4}''$	$\times\ 3\frac{1}{2}''$
LINEN No. 2	$11\frac{1}{2}''$	$\times\ 4\frac{3}{4}''$

Conclusion

Man's progress in understanding and ordering his environment has been illuminated by a succession of major discoveries. Making books must be counted as one of the most important steps towards civilisation and children's education must surely be reckoned incomplete if they are not allowed to meet and to master some of the problems that were encountered by those early craftsmen.

We have tried in this book to indicate the sorts of books which children like making, and can make well, and the part that such books can play in their education. The making of a book by a child whether it be a simple folded sheet of paper, or a collection of leaves stitched and bound in boards, calls upon a wide range of skills and combines them in a unique and purposeful enterprise.

There is far more to it than the development of technical expertise, however, for the essence of true craftsmanship is a blend of all those human qualities that teachers everywhere seek to encourage in their children. Learning to observe and to discriminate, to consider and compare, to exercise choice and to apply a consistent sense of standards to his endeavours is as necessary to the good craftsman as his dexterity with his tools.

In order to achieve both skills and attitudes, children need to work in a context that acknowledges these truths. The way in which a teacher arranges his classroom, and the relationship that he seeks to establish with his children are of first importance. As D'Alembert said, 'In a workshop it is the situation that is eloquent, not the craftsmen'.

It is our earnest hope that this book, written from our own experience and acknowledging the wisdom we have learned from others and now wish to pass on, will encourage many teachers to seek to release the remarkable powers of their children in this ancient and basic craft.

Index

tail 3